BETTER THAN A STICK IN THE EYE

A METHOD FOR RESOLVING CONFLICTS AND BRINGING ABOUT CHANGES IN MARRIAGES, FAMILIES, AND THE WORKPLACE

MERIDETH & AARON

I Hope you enjoy the Book

BY

ZIBA GRAHAM, JR.

authorHOUSE®

AuthorHouse™
1663 Liberty Drive
Bloomington, IN 47403
www.authorhouse.com
Phone: 1-800-839-8640

First published by AuthorHouse 8/3/2009

ISBN: 978-1-4389-8690-6 (e)
ISBN: 978-1-4389-8688-3 (sc)
ISBN: 978-1-4389-8689-0 (hc)

Library of Congress Control Number: 2009906108

Printed in the United States of America
Bloomington, Indiana

This book is printed on acid-free paper.

Dedicated to
the hundreds of people I have counseled who taught
me the resilience of the human spirit
and to all the people who will be helped by reading
this book

ACKNOWLEDGMENTS

This book, which has taken six years to complete, wouldn't have been possible without the support and advice from many people. Connie Gray encouraged me to go back to school at age fifty to get my master's in social work. When I worked at Catholic Charities in Evansville, Indiana, Jim Collins introduced me to short-term solution-based therapy, which started me out in counseling on a firm foundation. Also at Catholic Charities, I worked with Kristel Riffert who was always positive, supportive, and willing to share new ideas. Vickie Knowlden was my counseling partner at Life Coach, and I am grateful to her for helping me develop the ZG method. Emily Meier was one of the first to read over the manuscript, and I appreciate her suggestions and feedback.

My first editor, Jennifer Perrin, was extremely helpful in setting the book up in a logical fashion and was a taskmaster when I needed one. My brother John Graham stayed with me through the whole project and kick-started it more than once.

I am also grateful to my children and their spouses, Dan and Melissa Graham, Bridget and Dan Thuente, and Michael and Kara Graham, for their continuing support and timely suggestions. Tim Murphy, Anthony Schrock, and all the people at AuthorHouse were immensely helpful in getting the book into its final form, and I appreciate their time and support. And most of all, I want to thank my wife of thirty-nine years, Cathy, who has done all of the typing for me. Her steady support and encouragement made this project possible.

PREFACE

It is not the strongest of the species that survives, nor the most intelligent that survives. It is the one that is most adaptable to change.

—attributed to Charles Darwin

Sometimes living with conflicted relationships can seem as bad as a stick in the eye. The question then becomes, "What do you do about them?" Many people run from these conflicts by moving away, changing jobs, or divorcing. Others may try to live with the situation, hoping it will get better, and still others will try to resolve these conflicts by attempting to change the people involved. But what makes people open to change? Why do they sometimes persist in not changing when the evidence is compelling that they would be better off if they did change? What happens when a person who has failed to change for years suddenly changes for the better almost overnight? Why is it that some managers can have a workforce that is open and accepting about change, while others can't make their workers change no matter what they do? Why can some marriages survive tremendous change while others cannot? How is it that some parents can raise children who are open to change while other parents find resistance at every suggestion?

This book will help you answer these questions. It is about helping people resolve conflicts and change for the better. And in the process of helping others change, you will also change. Helping people change is a learned skill that anyone can master. It is a way of thinking and acting that allows change to come about. This is not a manipulative technique that makes people into what you want them to be, but rather a set of skills that enables you to help a person change to bring out the best in him. Although this change process is outward-oriented toward helping others, it will have a profound effect on the person who is the helper. Following the ZG method outlined in this book will help both you and the other person accept change and become better persons.

Helping people change presupposes that in some way they are open to change. Obviously, you can't help bring change about if the person absolutely refuses to even consider it. This is rarely the case, however, because change is the natural order of things, and staying the same often requires more energy than changing. In this book you will find ways to help your spouse/friend/coworker *want* to change along with you to allow a relationship that is satisfying and beneficial to you both.

CONTENTS

CHAPTER 1:

MY STORY

My story starts with a big change—a career change that I had been thinking about for quite some time. My work life had consisted of three years in the navy, mostly at sea; a master of business administration degree; and twenty-five years' experience running a family agricultural business in southwestern Indiana. At age fifty, I decided to leave the family business, go back to school, and get a master's degree in social work (MSW). It just seemed that everything came together so I had the time to pursue this change. Our three children were just finishing college, my wife Cathy was a junior college professor, and a succession plan was in place at the family business.

When I was in college and graduate school, I had focused on business classes and had no time for electives outside of the business school. Even though I always had an interest in taking some sociology and psychology courses, I never could because of my full schedule. Thus I was looking forward to trying a new field. I enrolled in a special program where I could take classes two full days per week, including nights. At the end of a year and a half, I received my MSW. After graduating, I worked for a social services agency for three years and then on my own as an independent counselor for seven years.

When I was planning my career change, I always thought I wanted to do mostly counseling, but after my first few counseling sessions, I became very disillusioned. I started out counseling the way I was taught. Basically it goes like this: The client comes in; the counselor says, "Tell me what is happening in your life"; the client talks for fifty minutes, sometimes nonstop; and then the counselor schedules another appointment. Over the course of many appointments, the counselor tries to listen, makes appropriate suggestions, and asks questions to help the client change. The clients keep coming back because somehow they think they feel better for having told their story to an impartial listener.

The first thing I discovered was that just telling their story didn't help clients to resolve their conflicts or change their lives. In fact, it seemed that telling about their broken relationships and all the other bad things in their lives created a barrier to their changing. It was almost as if they were giving themselves permission to be dysfunctional because of their terrible life history. For me, as a counselor who believed in positive change, this was a very sad experience.

Often, I would have clients, who were very successful professionals, come in for counseling because their marriage or other family relationships weren't working. They would come in with a hopeful, self-assured manner, but they would go out after fifty minutes looking sad and defeated because of the stress of reliving the tragic events in their lives. This scenario would play out over and over. After a few months of listening to all these tales of woe and seeing very little change, I began thinking I had made a big mistake in becoming a mental health counselor. The work was taking a heavy mental toll on me personally. Listening to people spill out all the bad stuff that ever happened to them, for hour after hour five days a week, was getting me down. It was endless, and my clients didn't change to make their relationships better, but they seemed to be getting worse. Just having a professional counselor listen to their stories seemed to reinforce their attitude of unwilling victim.

Not only was this a downer for me as someone who became a counselor to help people, but I found that they were becoming dependent on me. I was being asked to judge things the client said, such as "Should I put up with that?" "Shouldn't I have a life, too?" "What should I do when he says [this]?" "Should I confront her?" "How should I do that?" I discovered that clients have a tendency to become dependent on their counselor. This is why most counselors have an unlisted home telephone number.

There is nothing worse than for a counselor to get a phone call from a client who is in the middle of an argument with his spouse, asking what he should say next. This dependency can get bad enough that the client can't make the simplest decision without checking with his counselor. I once met a man who had been in marriage counseling for four years—with a standing appointment every Wednesday. I wondered to myself if he would continue going to any other helping professional for help for four years. If your medical doctor treated you once a week for two or three months and you weren't getting better, you would probably leave and try someone else.

Faced with this disappointing start to my counseling career, I knew I had to change my counseling methods or get out of the field altogether. Since this traditional method wasn't working, I started looking for a method that really worked. My previous professional experience had been focused on making things work. In the military, in business school, and in the agricultural business, I was constantly solving problems to help make things work better, cheaper, and faster.

Farmers, in particular, are very inventive and are quick to incorporate new ideas and products into their operations to make them work more efficiently. They have to be as efficient as possible because, as my grandfather used to say, "Farming is tough because farmers buy all their inputs at retail and sell their products at wholesale." Farmers also share any new innovations very freely with each other. This willingness to help a neighbor become more efficient is in great part because they aren't in competition with each other. If a nearby farmer produces an extra ten bushels more than you do, it doesn't affect the price you receive for your grain. After having spent about twenty-five years in many different aspects of the agricultural business, I was definitely in the "Do what works" mode—or "Keep trying different things until it does work" or "If it doesn't work, stop trying it and do something else" mode.

My counseling practice served the "worried well." The focus was on people who were mentally healthy but who were impacted by stressful life events and experiencing relationship difficulties within their marriage, family, or professional life. Since what I had been doing wasn't producing positive change in my clients, I determined what outcomes I wanted and then tried to devise a method of therapy that would produce these outcomes.

For starters, I wanted a way to measure outcomes so that both counselor and client could track the progress that the client was making. I also wanted a method that was positive and concentrated on the future instead of the past. This method also had to provide answers to problems instead of creating more problems and needed to bring results quickly because my clients couldn't afford the time or money for long-term therapy. This method needed to be structured and directed by the counselor, but the ideas for change should come from the clients. And finally, this method must result in both cognitive and behavioral changes and needed to produce independence for the client instead of a dependency on the counselor.

I found a lot of helpful tools in the work of Steve de Shazer, Insoo Kim Berg, and their colleagues at the Brief Family Therapy Center in Milwaukee, Wisconsin. In the creation of the solution-focused brief therapy approach during the 1980s, Shazer, Berg, and their team developed several ground-breaking therapeutic tools, such as the miracle question, scaling questions, and more.

After experimenting with various counseling tools, including parts of solution-focused brief therapy, I developed a way of approaching counseling that seemed to produce most of the outcomes that I wanted. I call this counseling approach the ZG method, and when I used it, I started to see real change in my clients. Many of the tools used to execute the method are borrowed from other successful therapies, bringing together the best techniques. The ZG method is a way of resolving interpersonal conflicts by helping to bring about changes in people and better their relationships.

Using the ZG method, most worried-well clients reported that their relationship conflicts diminished in severity after just two or three sessions, and usually after five sessions, they didn't need regular appointments anymore. By focusing on small, easily made adjustments that produce enormous differences in a rippling effect, the client can start to see change quickly.

- In order to measure outcomes, the ZG method uses self-reporting scales similar to the ones used in hospitals to communicate the severity of pain. Scaling questions use answers on a scale from one to ten, with the initial rating not as important as the direction and amount of change over time.

- The ZG method focuses on answers, not on problems. Instead of spending time discussing what the problem is or might be, the concentration is on the solutions that can be implemented so that the problems are solved or diminished. Focusing on answers helps to eliminate blame and creates a positive outlook.

- The ZG method also encourages the client to look to the future and envision how it will be when the problems are solved or become manageable. Rather than focusing on the past and rehashing old problems, clients can look to the future and adjust their life to how they want it to be. The past is not the future, so why dwell on it?

- Pushing faults and weaknesses aside, the ZG method stresses each person's unique strengths and gifts. People are helped to discover the areas where they excel and are encouraged to steer their energies in that direction.

- The ZG method is positive, focuses on the future, and encourages the client's independence rather than dependence on the counselor.

What a difference using this type of therapy made in my counseling life! Clients were upbeat and positive about where they were going instead of depressed about where they had been. And best of all, they could usually see real progress immediately, even after the first session. People were really changing and developing better relationships. They were becoming happy in their marriage again, and families were coming back together.

One big change for me, however, was that I kept getting the pink slip! Over and over, at the end of the third or fourth session, the person or couple I was counseling would say, "We seem to be getting along well enough that we don't need your services anymore." It was a great day for me when I got fired. I decided early on that I would try to help all clients resolve their difficulties as quickly as possible so they could become independent, fully functioning people again, and to see that happening was terrific.

With most of my individual clients getting better and not needing counseling anymore, I decided to try these counseling techniques in the workplace. Having been in the business world for twenty-five years, I knew that many times businesses are severely hampered by interpersonal conflicts. Like most business leaders, I somehow got through four years of business in college and a master's program but was never really taught how to solve interpersonal issues. We talked a lot about leadership and read all the books and essays, but we never really learned what to do when two vice presidents won't talk to each other or the bookkeeper won't accept the new person who was hired to do accounts payable.

Learning how to solve interpersonal conflicts in the workplace becomes more important the further up you go in the organization. And when you get to the top, your whole day is spent getting people to collaborate. All the technical expertise a person used to get up the ladder is now performed by someone else, and what remains is to figure out how to get Charlie and Debbie to work together.

When I applied this same ZG method in the workplace, I got similar results. People were able to get over their petty animosities and really work together. The setting would sometimes be different—mostly groups instead of one on one—but the results were excellent. I discovered that what works in marriages and families also works in businesses, factories, and institutions because, essentially, they are all the same—groups of people working together to get something done. They are all people with interpersonal conflicts, and they all need to mend their relationships.

When I retired from counseling, I wanted a way to share the ZG method with other people so they could use it in resolving their own conflicts and mending their own relationships. This book is the result of that desire to help people and share the accumulated wisdom of ten years talking to couples, families, bosses, and employees. The ZG method is a resource that is easy to learn and apply. It works quickly and effectively to bring people together and doesn't harm anyone. Most importantly, it helps people change for the better by allowing them to have control over the process and the solution. You will learn what to say, what not to say, and how to get unstuck, but discipline will be required to stay with this method and not slip back into old problem-blaming habits. What I have to offer you is hope—the hope and the possibility that things are going to get better when you use the ZG method. Having people use this method successfully to enhance their lives would complete this journey for me, which began fifteen years ago with my own change.

CHAPTER 2:

AN INTERACTIVE TOGETHER-HELP BOOK

Relationships are important. Throughout human history, people have realized that much more can be accomplished by working together than by working alone. The need for good working relationships became obvious to even our earliest ancestors. Human culture is built on relationships, because it is only by working together that a civilization can advance. As the world becomes more advanced, relationships become even more important, and they are always changing because the people are changing. That is why this isn't a "self-help" book, but rather a "together-help" book. In relationships, it is impossible to have only one person change. When one person changes, the relationship changes, and therefore the other person must change, too.

People get sick, go to school, change jobs, have children, get married, get old, and move away. Each time, their relationships change. One of the main reasons married couples came to see me for counseling was that through many years of change, they had simply drifted apart. This continual change is why relationships must be constantly tended and why it is very important to maintain good relationships, especially the high-stakes ones, such as marriages, families, and work. In order to be successful in life, you have to promote and maintain good, healthy relationships, but when a relationship stretches and strains over time, sometimes you are not sure how to get it back on track. This book is about helping relationships change for the better. Learning better relationship skills might be one of the most important things you do in your life!

As you read through this book, you will learn about the ZG method and how it is used to bring about change and resolve conflicts. You will learn the rationale behind the method so you can understand what is happening and why it works. You will also learn to demystify the process of change by realizing that much change is simply rediscovering what you already know. In addition, you will learn how to identify and let go of bad habits that are harming your relationships.

I once was counseling a man who was having marriage difficulties. When I suggested some things he might do to help make his marriage better, he replied, "I'm not going to do that because that is what she wants me to do." Obviously, he had a bad habit of simply resisting everything she wanted him to do.

Other chapters in the book will discuss the differences between solving problems and resolving interpersonal difficulties. Some of the information presented might seem counterintuitive, but I have seen this process work time and time again for a variety of people. The book will take you through a step-by-step tutorial so you can apply the ZG method in your own family and workplace. These chapters lead you through the relational interaction that will mend and strengthen your most important relationships. There are also suggestions for supporting the change and the improved relationship. As you read through the book, you will learn to trust in the process and let it work.

Ultimately, the ZG method works because it puts the participants in charge of the changes. You are not following an outsider's recommendations, but instead you are coming up with your own plans for change.

CHAPTER 3:

THE ZG METHOD

The ZG method of helping people change is needed because the old methods don't work any more. For one thing, people are different. People now want to have choices and be part of the decision-making process that affects them. They want to find their own solutions, and with a simple Internet connection, they have access to an incredible amount of information that helps them do that. In this fast-paced, wired world, they can't take the time for long, drawn-out counseling and have generally dismissed the Freudian, deterministic approach. When it comes to resolving conflicts and mending relationships, they want a method that is easy to understand, simple to do, quick, and effective.

The ZG method is all of that and more. All of the methods and tools I used in ten years of counseling are explained and adapted so that anyone can use them in his own setting to produce similar results. The principles and methods in this book are not necessarily new, but they are combined together in a unique way that produces the most effective results. Of course, use of the ZG method is limited to the worried well—

people who are mentally healthy, but having trouble with a relationship. This method is not a quick fix for people with serious mental disorders or addictions, or in severely abusive relationships.

To help solve interpersonal difficulties, a different way of thinking is required because the old problem-solving techniques won't work and even make the situation worse. With this new mind-set, a simple plan can be followed to resolve most of the conflicts or minimize their impact on the smooth functioning of an organization or family.

With the ZG method, you will learn how to do the following:

- Quantify the amount of improvement participants are seeking in the relationship through scaling questions

- Focus on solutions instead of problems

- Create a clear and detailed picture of the future as you want it to be

- Emphasize each individual's strengths

- Ask the right questions

- Use the ZG method at home and at work to resolve conflicts

- Stay positive throughout the entire process

The purpose of this book is to resolve conflicts and help people change so that their relationships work better. This relationship might be within a family, school, hospital, business, community, or marriage—the principles apply to all of these because they all have people working together. By following the principles and methods outlined in this book, you can begin to resolve your conflicts and help the people you care about change for the better.

CHAPTER 4:

UNDERSTANDING THE ZG METHOD

A New Way of Thinking

In order to bring about change in ourselves and our relationships, it is imperative that we embrace a new way of thinking about interpersonal difficulties. The most important step is in defining the difficulty. When the difficulty is with a thing, you call it a "problem," but when it is with people, it should be called a "conflict." The reason for this distinction is that two very different methods are used to help solve these two different difficulties.

When dealing with things, we have problems, and we use the scientific method to find the answer. The scientific method is the classical way most people are taught to solve problems; it is used very successfully by researchers, doctors, car mechanics, computer technicians, and crime scene investigators. Using this method, you first identify the problem and make a hypothesis as to what caused it. Then you try to fix it with a collection of data from the past, observations, and experiments. After that, you decide whether your solution worked, often relying heavily on experts to validate your findings. Through the whole process, the focus is on the problem.

For example, if you are having a problem starting your car in the morning, you take it to a mechanic, who will ask you some questions. The mechanic follows a systematic line of questioning to rule out certain causes and lead him to the correct diagnosis. The questions will all be centered toward finding the facts surrounding the starting problem. Some of the questions the mechanic might ask are "When does this problem occur?" "Does it happen only in the morning or only when the car is hot?" "What kind of gas do you use?" "Are your fluid levels okay?" "Have any warning lights come on?"

This series of questions is designed to break the problem down into its parts. In an effort to determine all the facts, the mechanic might refer to a manufacturer's report, which would point out any defects in cars similar to your car. To further identify the problem, your car might be hooked up to a computer, which would give several possible causes for the poor starting. After further testing, the expert mechanic discovers the problem and informs you of the solution. Then after the proper repair, your car is starting fine again.

To Solve Problems

The <u>focus is on the thing</u> with the problem. If, for example, a person's car won't start, the initial focus is on the car and not the person trying to start it.

<u>Use the scientific method.</u> This is a method of solving problems by going through certain steps until the problem is found.

<u>It is concerned mostly with facts</u>: When the car won't start and is towed to the garage, the auto mechanic will ask a number of questions to get the facts.

After the mechanic learns the facts, he will <u>study the past</u>. He might ask, "Has this ever happened before? When?" or "Have you had trouble with the engine running rough or noticed it was using an excessive amount of gas?" He might also inquire if the car was harder to start on cold days.

The next step is for the mechanic to <u>break the problem down into parts</u>. Among other things, he will look at and test the battery, check the wiring, see if the tank has gas, and check the alternator.

The mechanic will also <u>look for weaknesses</u> in the system. Maybe the battery is dying or the wiring has a worn spot. He also checks the auto manual for problems that the particular make and model might have.

At all times, the <u>focus is on the problem</u>. The mechanic isn't really concerned about how the owner feels about the car or if this happened before when the owner had a different car and lived in another city.

While the mechanic is trying to <u>identify the problem</u>, he might find that these particular cars were shipped from the factory with defective alternators.

So with this information, he can <u>get the right answer</u>. In this example, the right answer is to install a new alternator and charge the battery. And because the defective part was under warranty, the customer didn't have to pay for the repair.

Because of his training and expertise, the auto mechanic is the <u>expert who defines the problem</u> and acknowledges that there really is a problem.

Since he fixed the problem by installing a new alternator, he was also the <u>expert who had the solution</u>.

In this case, <u>the solution is invented</u> because it was worked out after the mechanic started working on the car.

This whole procedure of solving problems is <u>systematic</u>, where possibilities are raised and rejected until the solution is found.

As we just saw, a recap of the process used in solving problems is as follows:

Solving Problems

The focus is on things.
Use the scientific method.
It is concerned mostly with facts.
Go to the past and study.
Break the problem down into parts.
Look for weaknesses.
Focus on the possible problems.
Identify the problem.
Get the right answer.
An expert defines the problem.
An expert has the solution.
The solution is invented.
It is systematic.

This list of actions to take when solving problems must seem familiar. Some might argue with the order of the steps or say that some steps were omitted, but generally this is how most of us were taught to solve problems. However, when this process is used to solve interpersonal conflicts, it doesn't work and often makes the situation worse.

If, for example, a manager tries to solve a personnel problem using the scientific method, he might call a meeting with all the people involved and announce, "We have a problem. The last shipment was late."

As soon as he says this, everyone else in the room thinks, "Oh-oh, someone is in trouble, but it isn't me."

So right away, everyone is on the defensive. Then the manager brings up the "facts" of the case as he sees them and explains what happened. Again, many people in the room don't agree with his version of the facts, but they don't say anything because they don't want to draw attention to themselves. He then breaks the problem down and explains what happened to cause the late shipment. He traces the last shipment from the initial order through to the delivery, breaking apart each function. When he does this, everyone is thinking, "He is looking for a scapegoat—how can I cover my butt?"

If he questions anyone individually about what happened, they simply reply that they did their part in the process in an accurate and timely manner. So it couldn't have been them.

Then the manager says, "This has happened before, and we have a weakness here. I am going to get to the bottom of it, and heads will roll."

Now everyone is scared because the boss is on the warpath.

The manager then says, "Look, this isn't that hard," and he reviews the whole ordering/delivery process, explaining everything in great detail.

Now everyone is thinking, "That really isn't the way we do it anymore because we tried it that way, and it didn't work." The group is also thinking, "He doesn't even know how we are doing this now. If we go back to that old way, nothing will get out in time."

Now he starts asking questions about what everyone did in the process. But despite the asking and probing, he can't seem to "get to the bottom" of the problem. As the manager becomes increasingly frustrated, everyone else already knows who the problem is. The problem is Joe. Joe has been working in the shipping department for twenty years, and he is going to retire in two years. Recently, Joe's wife was diagnosed with cancer, and Joe has been so distracted that he forgets his medication or takes too much, which makes him more forgetful. The other guys in the shipping department have been covering for him as best they can, but this is the second time this week that Joe has "spaced out" and missed an order.

Everyone in the company really likes Joe. He has been like a grandfather to them and is always friendly and cheerful. Besides, they know this is only a temporary situation because his wife is on chemo and has a very good prognosis. No one says anything that would implicate Joe because they are afraid he would be fired. In the meantime, the manager is becoming increasingly upset because he is getting nowhere in trying to solve the "problem." In frustration, the manager ends the meeting, saying, "This better never happen again."

This type of meeting occurs countless times every day in work environments around the world, and it also happens with families and couples. Whether the conversation results in zipped lips like Joe's story or a downward spiral of finger pointing, it creates frustration, causes hard feelings, and doesn't solve the "problem." In fact, it usually makes it worse.

Anytime a "problem" comes up, the first thing to do is to identify whether it deals with things or people. If it deals with both things and people, treat it as if it is a people "problem." When finding a solution to people or interpersonal conflicts, rather than using the scientific method, which we have seen doesn't work, it is better to use the ZG method. The following is a breakdown of the ZG method, which is used to find solutions where people are involved.

Resolving Conflicts

In resolving conflicts, the <u>focus is on people</u>. If, for example, a couple is having marital difficulties, the focus is on them and not the car they drive or the house they live in.

To resolve these conflicts, the <u>ZG method is used</u>. This is a method designed to resolve interpersonal difficulties.

In these situations, the main <u>concern is with feelings</u>. Often when I was counseling, I would have to remind myself, "Now, don't let the facts get in the way." Facts aren't important. What is important is how the couple feels about the "facts." If she feels that his drinking four beers in the evening is too much, then it is a cause for concern. Likewise, if he feels she shouldn't spend more than one hundred dollars before checking with him, then that also is a cause for concern.

Instead of talking about the past, the ZG method helps the couple <u>go to the future and envision</u> what it will be like when they are getting along better. One important characteristic of a good relationship is that people often talk about their future interactions. When I would ask a couple what their day would be like if they were getting along perfectly, they would usually say that at some time, they would be planning future family events. Above all, stay out of the past, because it lays blame and hinders progress.

Rather than break the problem into parts, using the ZG method, <u>the conflict is left whole</u>. Interpersonal relationships are based on the feelings about all of the interactions that take place and not on one or two specific instances. If, for example, a couple has a healthy, positive marriage, a few minor disappointments won't severely damage that relationship.

Another important step to use in resolving conflicts is to <u>look for and emphasize strengths</u>. Stressing individual weaknesses is usually what leads to dysfunctional relationships in the first place. People know their own weaknesses better than anyone else, and having someone else point them out leads to resentment. Emphasizing the individual strengths of people improves relationships because it is the positive characteristics that bring people together.

It is important to <u>focus on the solution</u> and not on the problem. When dealing with interpersonal difficulties, no one really knows what the problem is, and trying to find out just causes antagonism and makes things worse. The key is to go to the solution. In the case of a marriage conflict, the solution is the answer to the question "If your marriage was perfect or a ten, what would be different?" Helping people to arrive at this solution is explained in detail in later chapters.

Identifying the solution is the first step in helping people really change. If they can see themselves and their spouse in this perfect marriage, for example, they have a model to imitate. The solution is for them to act as if they were in this perfect marriage.

To help people find the solution to their conflicts, it is necessary to ask the right question. The right question leads to the solution. Good questions help people think and then act. Later in the book, there is a chapter on how to ask the right questions, but for now it is important to note that having the right question is more important than having the right answer.

As mentioned before, the problem is not identified when helping to resolve interpersonal conflicts. When I did marriage counseling, I asked each person to describe in one sentence the difficulty that brought them to counseling. (Notice I didn't use the word "problem.") I only allowed them one sentence because I really didn't have to know their difficulty to help them find the solution.

In interpersonal conflicts, the solution is in the individual who has the difficulty. This person is the only one who can really find the solution to their own "problems."

This solution is discovered because it is already present in the person; the person is simply unaware of it. Sometimes this solution is rediscovered, in that it has been used before and then forgotten.

Rather than going from step to step in a systematic process, the ZG method results in enlightening moments that become a process of discovery.

As a recap, here is the outline for solving interpersonal conflicts.

<u>Resolving Conflicts</u>

The focus is on people.
Use the ZG method.
The concern is with feelings.
Go to the future and envision.
The conflict is left whole.
Look for strengths.
Focus on the solution.
Identify the solution.
Get the right question.
The problem is not identified.
The solution is in people.
The solution is discovered.
It is a process of discovery.

This list might seem a bit strange to a person who has always used the scientific method to solve problems, but it has been my experience that when the ZG method is used, people change quickly and easily, and find solutions to their conflicts. The basic differences between the scientific method and the ZG method revolve around getting the facts, going to the past, and asking questions.

Using the previous example of the late shipments, the outcome would be very different when using the ZG method. The manager might open the meeting by saying, "I was thinking of things we might do to ensure that we don't have any late deliveries. I would appreciate your input and thought we would start asking ourselves some questions. What if our order/delivery system was the best it could possibly be—let's say it was a ten. If this happened, what would be different? How would it feel different to work here?"

One of the workers answers, "Well, for one thing, if we were a ten, we wouldn't be so worried about a late shipment because there wouldn't be any."

The manager asks, "Then what would you be doing with the time you spend worrying?"

"I guess I would be concentrating on my job more," the worker says.

The manager asks another worker what else would be different if the department was a ten or the best it could be.

The worker answers, "I guess we would be more like a team. For instance, when someone got behind or needed a little extra help, another person would cut their break short and pitch in."

Another worker says, "Yeah, I think the rule we have that you can't leave your area is dumb."

The manager asks, "What would be happening differently if that rule wasn't there anymore?"

Another worker says, "We all know how to do each other's jobs, and if we help out just a little in another department when we aren't busy, things would go a lot smoother."

At this point, all of the workers are thinking that it is a dumb rule. They know this because they talk about it at lunch and discuss how, without the rule, they would be much more efficient with fewer errors.

The manager asks, "Okay, let's say the rule was taken out. How would this department look and run differently?"

A worker replies, "Well, I can see how this might work. For example, I work in packaging and when we get the day's shipments packaged and moved to shipping, we only have to sweep up, and I have time to help someone else. The other day, we were just standing around, and I looked over at Joe in shipping and saw a big pile he had to work through before quitting time. I could have gone over and helped him and still had my place cleaned up in time."

The manager asks if anyone else had ideas about how it would work if the rule was changed. Another worker replies, "I work in sorting, and we are busiest in the morning and shipping isn't very busy then. Maybe Joe and some of the guys in shipping could help us then and we could help them later."

The manager asks, "Are there any other ideas about what would be different if we did this?"

Another worker says, "The way it is now, we are really busy part of the time and waiting for product the rest of the time. If we could pitch in and work together as a team, we could get the whole job done on time and we wouldn't be so stressed out."

Another worker adds, "Lunch break would be a lot calmer and more relaxed."

Another worker chimes in, "Maybe we would even laugh at Joe's jokes again."

The manager then says, "Thank you all for coming today. I appreciate your input. You all can go back to your jobs now."

After hearing the workers' recommendations, the manager decides to let the workers implement the changes they suggested. The manager knows that the workers will try their best to make the system work better with their new changes in place.

The question is, which manager would you rather work for? The first manager, who used the scientific method, created defensiveness, fear, and unease in his group, while the second manager, using the ZG method, saw the creation of a sense of teamwork in his group. The second manager asked the workers to visualize a future where the system was the best it could be and knew that the workers would discover the solution. He also knew that if the workers discovered the solution, they would be much more likely to make it work than if it came from him.

He knew that if he just asked the right questions, they would discover the right answers. He intentionally did not try to find fault, look for weaknesses, or go into the past.

When dealing with interpersonal difficulties, it is always best to use the ZG method. When dealing with interpersonal conflicts, you can't ever get all the true facts because they are self-reported. Likewise, you can't identify the "problem" because it is also subjective. In these situations, people don't want to focus on the past because it brings up guilt, bad feelings, and finger pointing. Questions are used, not to discover what happened, but rather to help people think about how it is going to be when the solution has been discovered.

Following is a recap of the two methods, listed together for comparison:

Scientific Method	ZG Method
You have a problem.	You have a conflict.
The focus is on things.	The focus is on people.
It is concerned mostly with facts.	The concern is with feelings.
Go to the past and study.	Go to the future and envision.
Break the problem down into parts.	The conflict is left whole.
Look for weaknesses.	Look for strengths.
Focus on the possible problems	Focus on the solution.
Identify the problem.	Identify the solution.
Get the right answer.	Get the right question.
An expert defines the problem.	The problem is not identified.
An expert has the solution.	The solution is in people.
The solution is invented.	The solution is discovered.
It is systematic.	It is a process of discovery.

When resolving any difficulty, it is essential to first classify it as either a problem or a conflict. If it is a problem involving things, you solve it by using the scientific method. If it is a conflict involving people, you resolve it by using the ZG method.

Find the Solution

As we have seen, in traditional problem-solving situations, the first step is to identify the problem. However, when developing the skills to resolve personal conflicts, it isn't necessary or even desirable to identify the problem first. In most interpersonal conflicts, no one can identify the problem, and usually the participants will disagree on what the problem really is. Many times, outside experts are brought in to identify the problem, but they don't really know either. If more than one expert were consulted, they would probably have different opinions.

In many cases, when a marriage, family, or business relationship isn't working, someone determines what the problem is, and then the people involved are asked to change in order to solve the problem. This process doesn't work for many reasons. For example, it may be that the people can't agree on what or who the problem is, or they might not even agree that there is a problem. And if the individuals involved do agree on the problem, they often don't agree on the solution, or they may think that the solution won't work. This type of attempt at solving interpersonal conflicts is a failure from the start and can actually lead to more resistance and worse relationships.

When problems are stated, people tend to focus on them instead of focusing on the solutions. When this happens, problems usually get much bigger and a lot more complicated. Whole meetings are spent trying to understand the depth and complexity of the "problems," until the whole organization or family is under an all-encompassing problem cloud.

When this happens, the solutions also get larger and more complex. This continues until the solutions become impossible to implement. During this process, the mood of all the participants continues to decline, and the objective becomes saving your own skin and not being identified as part of "the problem." This is where the finger pointing starts and chaos reigns.

Into this confusion and disarray steps "the boss" who makes an arbitrary decision. Rather than arriving at a collaborative solution, the boss, parent, or individual with the most power dictates what the solution will be. Consequently, the participants feel that they have been dealt with in a very arbitrary manner and are generally unhappy with the decision. The result is unhappy people forced to change and giving the minimum to their work, family, or marriage.

The preceding scenario is the way most people try to solve interpersonal problems, and it hardly ever works to the satisfaction of the people involved. Sometimes, it seems to work for a short time, but down deep, people are only going through the motions to keep their job or keep peace in the family. The only real answer is to ignore the problem and focus on the solution.

When I first started in marriage counseling, I would ask a couple what problem in their marriage brought them to see me. The wife would usually start by rolling her eyes and then launch into a litany of things her husband did that she didn't like: not communicating enough, going out too much, not helping enough with the kids, spending too much money, and not wanting to spend time with her family. Then, I would turn to the husband, and he wouldn't see a problem. He would proceed to refute each complaint on his wife's list with a logical explanation. This type of exchange could go on for the whole fifty-minute appointment. Each person would have a unique view of the situation, and I was asked to take a side. They would say things like, "Don't you think that is a little extreme?" or "That's no big deal, right?" or "He [The counselor] knows that all guys do that." I quickly found out that it became a contest to see who could get me on their side so that person would have the stronger argument on the way home.

Many times, this conversation to "find the problem" would take up not only the whole first session but subsequent sessions as well. So many new problems kept coming up that it became impossible to keep track of all of them, let alone address each one. I came to two conclusions. The first was that the real problem can never be found. After all, if they didn't know what the problem was, how could I possibly know? The second was that it wasn't necessary to find it to discover the solution. After coming to these conclusions, I altered the way I did counseling. I discovered that focusing on the problem just made it bigger, while focusing on the solution seemed to make the problem smaller. In individual counseling, focusing on the problem too much makes it get bigger and can take it from "the problem" to "my problem" to "I am the problem." When this happens, the individual can slip into a kind of helpless depression, from which it is hard to recover.

When working with individuals in these types of situations, I try to not even use the word "problem." Words are powerful, and even a slight reference to a problem will start an automatic negative response in the individual. Using other words such as "issues," "difficulties," "situations," or "conflicts" seems to convey the message without saying the word "problem."

During an initial session with a couple, I would ask what their main difficulty was, and they would usually say "lack of communication." Later in the session, I would ask them to imagine that their marriage was a "ten," or a marriage that was as good as it could possibly be. Then I would say, "If your marriage actually was a ten, what is the first thing your spouse would say to you in the morning?"

Invariably, they would reply that if their marriage was a ten, the first thing their spouse would say would be, "Good morning."

When I would ask, "What would your reply be?" they would say, "Well, I would say 'Good morning' back."

So without discussing the details of the communication difficulty, this couple knew how good communication starts off in the morning. Instead of "he won't listen" and "she talks too much," the couple goes right to the solution.

When I did marriage counseling, I asked this same initial question of hundreds of couples, and almost all responded the same way—that a lack of communication was their main difficulty. Now when I do marriage enrichment programs, I stress that all couples should start the day with what I call the "McDonald's Minimum." When you walk into McDonald's in the morning, they say, "Good morning. How can I help you?" If every married couple said that to their spouse in the morning, I think the divorce rate would go down. This is a somewhat simplistic comparison, but it starts the process. In fact, the solution in all interpersonal difficulties is always the same. The solution is the answer to the question "If your relationship was a ten, or the very best it could be, what would you be saying, doing, hearing, thinking, and feeling differently?"

We usually get what we focus on. Just as the racecar driver focuses on the track and not the wall, we must focus on what we want and where we want to go. The key, then, is to focus on solutions instead of problems. The solution is for the persons involved to create an interaction where the problem is not present or is so minor that it is insignificant. To help people change, it is important to help them focus on these solutions. The remainder of this book will be on identifying and implementing these solutions.

Go to the Future and Envision

When I first started in mental health counseling, I just assumed that people would tell me all about their past and that somehow this would help them change. This would be especially true, or so I thought, if they could pinpoint the reason for their problems. This cathartic purging of their innermost feelings and thoughts would surely bring about great change once they understood where the problems stemmed from.

After spending many hours with all types of clients, I discovered that catharsis doesn't bring about change. Actually, it often prevents change. Sometimes, people will fixate on a past disturbing event, and this fixation becomes the reason they can't ever change. Thinking and talking about these negative past events diminish people's spirits, lock them into the past, and prevent progress. Describing the particular event to a professional counselor makes it even larger and more of a determining factor in their life. In my experience, dwelling on past negative, hurtful experiences usually doesn't help a person change and only makes change harder. The only time it is helpful to relive the past is when people describe a positive experience. In this case, it can sometimes help them to re-create a solution that worked in the past.

When reviewing a person's past history, a counselor can highlight a particular event, and suddenly it grows from a seemingly insignificant happening into a real problem. Often a person comes out of counseling with more "problems" than when he started.

Another outcome, when clients share their past, is that they get a diagnosis. Now, not only do they have more intimidating problems, but they also have a mental disorder. They are labeled with a mental illness, which is someone's best judgment based on reported symptoms. This is quite different from a diagnosis based on test results that can be replicated and confirmed by an outside source. As in all types of diagnoses, regardless of if it is correct or not, when it is entered into the permanent record, it is there forever. Once labels are attached to people, it is sometimes difficult for them to ever see themselves as mentally healthy again. The old label holds them down and prevents them from changing. Past negative events pull people down and prevent them from visualizing who they want to be.

Another way this past history keeps people from changing is that their medical file precedes them everywhere they go. When taking on a new client, it is customary for the counselor to review the file before ever seeing the client. This sometimes biases the counselor.

For this reason, I made it a point to never read the old chart when I got a new client. Enough information can be uncovered in the first session to have an adequate understanding of the situation. This same effect of the negative past preventing change is present in families, schools, and the workplace. People remember what family members did when they were children and hold it against them. In schools, teachers warn the next teacher in line about the troublemakers. In the workplace, an individual sometimes has to change employers in order to move up because the boss sees that person as incapable of a more challenging job. In all of these examples, the person in charge is holding back change by labeling a person based on past experience.

It has been fashionable to argue about what makes a person who they are. Most discussions revolve around the nature versus nurture theories. Are people a result of their genes (nature) or their upbringing (nurture)? Regardless of which theory is right, a person's image of himself is an important component in what makes a person who he is. This image is very powerful and is necessary for positive change to happen. I have seen people change almost overnight when they forget the old image they have had in the past and start seeing themselves as they want to be in the future.

When people can see themselves and their relationships as they will be after their difficulties are gone, they are on the road to recovery and change. The more detailed this vision of themselves is, the more powerful it becomes as an agent of change and the more it overwhelms any past difficulties.

I counseled a man who was having marital difficulties, which were based on his idea that he was somehow tricked into getting married. He grew up in a small country town and then enlisted in the army. During the course of his army travels, he met a sophisticated city girl, and they were married after a whirlwind courtship. Despite the fact that he now resided in a large city and had become a very successful general manager for a large corporation, he always felt that he was a country bumpkin who had been taken advantage of by his wife. When he was able to see himself as a sophisticated, big-city, upper-management businessman, his view of his marriage changed also. He was no longer the bumpkin, but a willing participant on the same level with his wife. When this occurred, he was able to repair his marriage and family.

Negative views of the past aren't beneficial. They keep people from changing themselves and don't allow others to accept positive changes in people. On the contrary, positive views of the future are more powerful than negative experiences of the past and allow people to change. The tool I found most useful for implementing the envisioning process is the miracle question. The miracle question comes from the solution-focused brief therapy approach, developed by de Shazer and Berg. It asks participants to envision a specific future free from their current issues. The miracle question is as follows: "If a miracle happened tonight while you were sleeping and all the problems in your relationship were suddenly resolved, what would be different tomorrow?" Participants are asked to describe this "perfect miracle day" in great detail. Additional queries "milk" the miracle question and reveal how parts of the miracle might already be happening.

In describing their miracle day, people set out a blueprint of what they want to see happen. Now, they can start working toward that vision.

Ask the Right Questions

A few years ago, I was talking with a college administrator. During the course of the conversation, he stated that his job was to just ask the right questions. When he first said this, I thought, "What a cop-out that is! Here is a man who is paid to run a college, and, instead of having the answers, all he has are the questions!"

After a few years as a counselor and consultant, I realized that he was right. When you tell someone the answer, they respond in one of three ways: Either they agree, they disagree, or they are ambivalent. Their verbal, knee-jerk response will tend to be immediate. Giving an answer doesn't promote thought; it only elicits a verbal reaction.

When you ask a question, however, there is a tendency for the person to think first. Questions promote thinking, and good questions promote deep thinking. Sometimes, when a particularly good question is asked, there will be quite a long pause before the answer comes. This indicates that the person is very intent on thinking it through before replying. In helping people change, it is more important to ask questions than to have the answers. The right questions help people discover their own answers and solutions. This shows respect for the person by acknowledging that he has the solution to his own difficulty. When people are encouraged to think and find their own solutions, they are more likely to follow through and change their behavior.

When I started counseling, I had an answer for every problem. The answers to other people's problems always seem so simple and obvious. Every problem had a ready-made solution, and like Ann Landers, I just had to quote the reigning expert or just use common sense. After explaining the solution, I would give the clients some homework to do for the next session.

This method, however, didn't work very well. There was no change occurring in the relationship, and the clients seldom completed any of the homework I had assigned.

I finally figured out that most of this obvious advice I was dispensing had been given to them many times before they came into counseling. I was just repeating the same solutions they had heard from their parents, siblings, spouse, or trusted friends. They didn't take the advice from them, so why should they take it from me? When it became obvious that this type of counseling wasn't working, I stopped having all the answers and started asking questions.

When asking questions, though, it is important to ask the right ones. All questions must be free from a controlling attitude on the part of the person asking the questions. Never, never start a question with "why"! "Why" questions most often refer to the past and contain some connotation of blame or fault finding. The question "Why did you do that?" stirs up immediate resistance in the person being questioned. Stay away from similar questions like "What were you thinking?" and "Don't you see what is happening here?" Good questions also lead people to discover their own answers and solutions. Helping people find solutions by just asking them questions can be very frustrating at times, but the key is to persist with the sure knowledge that the solution is really present, just waiting to be found. When people are encouraged to think and find their own solutions, they are more likely to follow through and change their behavior.

Questions that refer to the past should be avoided, except when they refer to positive or pleasant past events. It wouldn't be appropriate to ask, "What were you thinking when you got in trouble yesterday?" It would be proper, however, to ask, "What did you do yesterday to get such a good report from your teacher?"

When I counseled married couples, I sometimes found it helpful to ask, "Can you tell me about a time when you were really getting along as a couple?"

Once, I was counseling a couple whose vision for the future included more communication. When I asked them to describe, in great detail, a time when they talked more, they both agreed that communication had not been a problem when they lived on Elm Street and had a hot tub. Every night after the children were in bed, they would soak in the hot tub and talk for twenty or thirty minutes. The right questions led them to find their own solution to part of their conflict.

Despite all I have said about the ZG method, it is still hard to understand how this process works to bring about change when it consists of questions and not answers. I have a story that might help illustrate the process.

One day, I went to see a magic show. During the performance, the magician called for a volunteer from the audience, and a young man stepped up to the stage. The magician took out a deck of cards, fanned them face down in front of him, and asked the volunteer to pick any card and place it face down on a nearby table without looking at it. Then the magician put the remainder of the cards away and started asking the man questions:

Magician: What are the four suits?

Man: Spades, hearts, diamonds, and clubs.

Magician: Name two of those.

Man: Spades and hearts.

Magician: What are the other two?

Man: Diamonds and clubs.

Magician: Pick one of those.

Man: Clubs.

Magician: What is the other one?

Man: Diamonds.

Magician: Okay, diamonds it is. Remember diamonds. Can you remember diamonds?

Man: Yes I can.

Magician: Okay. What are the face cards?

Man: Jack, queen, and king.

Magician: Okay, what are the other cards?

Man: The other cards are ace through ten.

Magician: Okay, pick five of those.

Man: Ace through five.

Magician: Okay, pick three of those.

Man: Ace, two, three.

Magician: What are the other two?

Man: Four and five.

Magician: Pick one of those.

Man: Four.

Magician: Okay, you said four, correct?

Man: Yes, four.

Magician: Okay. What was the suit of cards I asked you to remember?

Man: It was diamonds.

Magician: Okay then, you said a four of diamonds. Is that correct?

Man: Yes, the four of diamonds.

Then the magician, with great flourish, picks up the card that was face down on the table, hands it to the man, and asks him to show it to the audience and tell them which card it is. The man looks at it, shows it to the crowd, and says, "It's the four of diamonds." The audience applauds. As the man is returning to his seat, he turns to the magician and asks, "How did you do that?" The magician just smiles and proceeds on to his next trick.

The answer to how he did it, like most magic tricks, is fairly simple. When the magician pulled out his deck of cards, he didn't show them to the audience because every card in the deck was the four of diamonds. The magician knew what card the man had chosen, and now with the right questions, he could lead the man to the right answer. When asked to name two of the four suits, the man said spades and hearts, but not diamonds, so the magician simply asked for the other suits. Then when the man still didn't choose diamonds, but chose clubs, the magician simply asked him what suit remained. Then the man had to guess correctly by naming diamonds. The magician repeated this same style of questioning to lead the man to the four. When the man saw the card, he couldn't believe he had guessed the four of diamonds correctly out of all of those cards.

The ZG method works somewhat like this old magician's trick. The magician knows the answer in the beginning, and, with the ZG method, so do you. The answer in the ZG method is always the same, namely that the relationship is a ten, or the best it can be. The questions lead you to describe what it will be like when your relationship is a ten. Along the way, you relate what it will feel like, sound like, and look like when the relationship is a ten. You will describe what other people will be doing and how you will interact with each other. When it is finished, the person answering the questions will have uncovered the answer without much effort.

Obviously, there is more to helping a person change than the trick I described, but it shows that if you know the answer and ask the right questions, the person will discover the magic on his own.

The Solution Is in People

The ZG method is based on the premise that the person who has the difficulty also has the solution, which acknowledges that he is the expert in his own particular situation. In interpersonal conflicts, the solution must be discovered and put into effect in an individual way to solve the difficulty. Consider how sometimes other people's problems seem to have such obvious solutions. If the solution is so obvious to us, why isn't it obvious to them? The answer lies in the fact that you can't solve other people's interpersonal difficulties; only the people involved can solve them.

Anyone who has been through counseling has probably been given homework or suggestions on how to rectify the situation. Invariably, they don't do the homework, don't follow the advice, or just go through the motions. The inescapable fact is that, in order to work, the solution must be discovered and put into place by the people experiencing the difficulty. This is the only way to have real ownership of the situation. No other person can possibly know the interactions that have transpired between the individuals experiencing the conflict. The solutions will be as unique as every interpersonal relationship.

I was counseling a young couple who had been married for about five years and complained of lack of communication and drifting apart. Because they were having trouble imagining their relationship going smoothly, I asked them to recall a time in the past when they were happier. They both agreed that they were very happy during the first two years of their marriage, but since then, they had drifted apart. I asked them what was different about those first two years that made them happy. There was a long silence, and I could tell that they were both trying to recall what was special about those first years. Finally, he looked at his wife and said, "Lotion."

She grinned. He grinned. They both looked at me, and I said, "Oh, lotion." Since the session was about finished, they made another appointment and left. A few days before their scheduled appointment, she called and said they were getting along much better now and didn't think they needed to see me anymore. I never did find out exactly what he meant when he said "lotion," but it seemed to be part of their solution. The answer was there. It was always there, just waiting to be discovered.

This was one of those magical moments when both individuals understood that the solution had been found. Like many solutions, this one was very individualistic and intimate, and could be known only by the individuals involved. The key is to always try to draw out the solution that will be recognized by all involved as the answer, or maybe as a possibility.

Most times when the solution is discovered, it doesn't seem to relate in any direct way to the "perceived problem." This is why, as I stated previously, the "problem" doesn't need to be identified. The ZG method allows people to find the solution within themselves—their solution.

CHAPTER 5:

LAYING THE GROUNDWORK FOR SUCCESS

Be Willing to Change Yourself

Helping others change starts inside you with a firm desire to change yourself. Sometimes, this means doing something that you have avoided or just put off for a long time. Part of this process is to be the best that you can be—the best parent, child, worker, or boss. Usually, we don't live up to our own ideal. My grandfather, who was involved with agriculture for many years, always said, "Nobody farms as well as they know how because something always seems to get in the way." The farmer who starts out with high hopes in the spring ends up adjusting his tillage and planting practices around the weather, machinery repairs, time constraints, government programs, and the availability of capital.

Like the farmer, we find that something always seems to get in the way of our living up to our full potential in our relationships. Most everyone knows how to be better at what they do. The trouble lies in just doing it. We recognize this about ourselves and seem to make allowances when grading our own performance in relationships. When it comes to other people, however, we usually aren't as willing to give them the benefit of the doubt. We usually judge ourselves by our intentions, but we judge others by their actions.

We can easily justify our actions (or our inaction). We think, "I did the best I could," "She understands that I really didn't mean it that way," or "With my job demands, I can't spend more time with the kids." In our minds, these are all valid reasons why we don't perform up to the standards we know. This reaction is, to some extent, our way of coping with the world and all the demands that work, family, and community place on us. The most important thing to recognize is that the person we are helping to change also feels this same way and must be allowed the same validations why their performance wasn't as good as it could have been. We must judge others in light of the "other things that got in the way."

Just as you know yourself better than anyone else, your loved ones or co-workers know themselves better than you do. They know what gets in their way and what it would be like if they could live up to their standard. Sometimes, <u>you</u> are one of the things that get in the way of another person doing their best.

When I counseled married couples who had been arguing, I always told them to say, "I'm sorry," even if the other person was wrong. This firm conviction that "I am right" has started more arguments than anything else.

Helping people change starts with the idea that maybe others know more than you do. Maybe they know how to do something better or more efficiently, which you didn't even think about. Maybe they understand the situation better than you do, and <u>you</u> are the roadblock to progress. These are humbling thoughts, but this mind-set is necessary to bring about change.

41

We must see ourselves as part of the conflict. Trying to change others because they are the cause of the conflict won't work. This just brings about resistance. It is a frightening thing to let someone help you change. It feels like we are losing control and not in charge. Usually when we give up control, it is because we have no choice. We do this when we fly in an airplane or go to the hospital for an operation. Even more so, voluntarily giving up control when we don't have to can be very uncomfortable.

To be willing to change or allow yourself to be changed when there is no outside pressure to do so is one of the hardest things a person can do in his lifetime. Change that is forced on us is generally rejected, but there is usually a penalty for rejecting it. If the highway department lowers the speed limit and I do not change my speed to comply, I will get a ticket. If the penalties are severe enough, behavioral changes can be elicited. But even if people comply, it doesn't mean that they accept the change. They just accept the behavior that protects them from the penalty. In this example, where change involves coercion or outside pressure, individuals may not agree with the change and concentrate on doing the minimum to not get caught speeding instead of obeying the spirit of the law. We often don't see ourselves as part of the problem, so why change?

To help another person change, you have to be willing to change. They cannot change unless you change, too. True, long-lasting change cannot occur unless both people change.

Be Aware that People Don't Usually Resist Change

It seems fashionable to think that people are usually resistant to change and that they hate change. This attitude stems from the realization that much of the time, when we try to change someone, we fail. We all have had the common experience where we try to change the behavior of our spouse, our children, or the people we work with and fail miserably. This experience can be extremely frustrating and leads us to the erroneous conclusion that people simply don't want to change.

In reality, most people only resist change when they perceive that it isn't in their best interest to change. Suggestions for change that come from someone else are usually resisted when the benefits are more in favor of the person giving the suggestion. No matter how much someone wants a person to change "for their own good," there is usually some benefit in it for him. If not, why would he have bothered with an attempt to change the other person in the first place?

Parents talk about being "worried to death" about their children using drugs. Obviously, if their children stopped using, the parents wouldn't worry any more. The same is true for a wife who wants her husband to stop speeding and to wear his seat belt. She gets "scared to death" when he isn't there and the phone rings. She imagines that the caller will be the police informing her that her husband has been in a serious accident.

When appeals for change fall on deaf ears, the person trying to initiate the change tends to repeat the request more often and more strongly, but these tactics simply make the other person more resistant. The more a person feels forced to change, the less real change will come about. When enough pressure and coercion is exerted upon a person, he will change, but only minimally enough to take off the heat.

In another scenario, you can have a person who outwardly goes along with the change, but quietly sabotages the change just to prove someone else wrong. This happens every day in families, in the community, and in the workplace. Instead of people working together, there is chaos. In families, it leads to disagreements, constant nagging, and unwanted behavior. In communities, it leads to power plays, division, and adversarial relationships. In the workplace, it leads to distrust, adversity, and a lack of commitment.

Because most people don't know how to help people change, they resort to pressure tactics, short-term incentives, or coercive punishments, all of which prevent real change from taking place. This failure leads people to conclude that others are highly resistant to change.

The truth is that people are very willing to change when they can see that it benefits them. If the tax code changes with a new tax credit, wouldn't an individual take advantage of it? If the state builds a new road that would cut fifteen minutes off of a person's daily commute, wouldn't that person change his or her route to work? Most people adopt change by purchasing the latest time-saving appliance or new, faster computer and by reacting to the latest trends and fashions in eager anticipation of the next new idea.

What if you could envision the next new idea in your relationship? With the ZG method, you can. Using the ZG method removes common barriers to change, such as fear and mistrust. The ZG method is often not about change, but about rediscovering those things that the person did that worked before. The ZG method puts people in charge of the change so they are comfortable with it, and not just doing what another person recommends. Individuals come up with plans for change that they think will work and that may have worked before. The ZG method removes the victim mentality and instead looks at individuals as capable people who are in charge of their own future.

Be Ready to Accept the Changes in Others

One of the biggest barriers to change is when a person who says he wants a change in a relationship won't let the other person change. I observed this many times in marriage counseling.

Usually, it was the wife who wanted her husband to change. This process could be especially difficult because of the different ways men and women change.

Women are very relational, and the time and effort they put into each relationship is carefully thought out. If one of their current relationships changes or a new one starts, all the existing relationships must be adjusted. This happens most glaringly when a woman has a baby. All her other relationships are adjusted with the arrival of that tiny person. Because of this characteristic, change for women happens slowly and more thoughtfully.

Men, however, change differently. They focus on only one thing at a time, and relational importance isn't well thought out. When they focus on that one thing, all other things are excluded, and change can happen very fast—almost instantly.

Why does this matter? In marriage counseling, these different timelines for change usually lead to the following situation: When the man suddenly realizes that his marriage and family relationships are in jeopardy, he focuses on repairing these relationships and usually changes instantly. Even though his wife has been asking, hoping, and praying for these changes for years, she is reluctant to accept this new man because of past experiences.

To her, it seems phony because "nobody could change that fast." She doesn't know how to react and feels manipulated by his actions. In the past, the changes only lasted a short time before he backslid again, and if she believes him, she could be hurt again.

Often, she is angrier now than before he changed. If it was so easy for him to change, why did he put her through so much grief for so many years? When he sees her negative reaction, he might revert back to his old ways, and it becomes a self-fulfilling prophecy. Ironically, just as he is really starting to work on the marriage relationship, she has stopped. The key is for him to persevere in the changes for a period of time so she knows they are permanent.

A couple of stories might illustrate this best. A man told me about a time when his wife was away on a business trip for a few days. She called him on her cell phone when she was about an hour from the house. Excited about her return, he cleaned the whole house, put fresh flowers on the table, and even had snacks and a chilled glass of wine ready for her. When she drove up, he went out to greet her, carried her luggage into the house, invited her to sit down and have some wine, and asked her about the trip. She sat down, took a sip of wine, looked around, and with a bemused look on her face, said to him, "Who are you and what have you done with my husband?"

In another instance, I had a woman come to counseling because her recently retired husband was driving her crazy. One day while she was out, he decided to be helpful and empty the laundry basket. He carefully folded everything and put it all away in the proper drawers. When she came home, she asked where the laundry was, and he told her what he had done. She said, "That was dirty laundry waiting to be washed. I can't believe you did that. I'll do the laundry as always." Instead of encouraging him in the change to help out around the house, she squelched any initiative he might have.

Many times, one person does something that shows that he is really trying to change for the better, and the other won't accept it. The attempt is rejected with "You are just doing that because the counselor told you to" or "You are just trying to stop a divorce." Faced with this rebuff, the person making the attempt usually gives up, thinking, "Well, at least I tried." Most people judge others on their past behavior, not a recent change. For a relationship to improve, everyone involved has to accept new, positive changes when they appear and leave the past in the past.

Be Principled in Your Change Process

In helping people change, it is absolutely imperative that none of the parties have preconceived agendas. Sometimes, it is difficult to determine what change for the better would entail, and there is always room for disagreement. The most important principle is to always let the people involved decide to change on their own, without any coercion. It must be their solution and their decision to change. Sometimes, they may decide not to change, and that has to be an acceptable decision.

Another principle is to do no harm. This is a guiding principle in the health care professions, and it should apply in helping people change as well. Other principles include treating people with love, patience, kindness, and honesty. The ZG method should be used with the other person's best interests at heart.

The test of whether the person has changed in a positive way is simple. Is the person happier, more confident, and more independent? Is he wiser and better able to make good decisions? Is he able to make and continue in healthy relationships that are mutually beneficial? If these questions can be answered in the affirmative, then the change has been for the better.

As I have discussed, change works best when it isn't forced upon people. There must be openness to the process that allows individuals to find solutions on their own. Pursuing preconceived solutions will be a setup for failure, and the process will become just another story of a person with power trying to force change on subordinates. Obviously, in cases where there is a power differential, bosses and employees, for example, or parents and children, everyone involved knows who has the last word, but people greatly appreciate a chance to arrive at their own solutions.

CHAPTER 6:

SAMPLE QUESTIONS

In the preceding chapters, we have examined the theory behind helping people resolve their conflicts, learned that the problem doesn't have to be known in order to find the solution, and discovered that a positive vision of the future is more powerful than a negative experience in the past. We also discovered that people can more easily change if they see a benefit for themselves and if they have a say in determining their future. In Chapter 4, I discussed the importance of asking the right questions. In this chapter, I go beyond the theory to direct action, because asking the right questions is what makes the ZG method work. In Chapters 7 and 8, you will be given exact details of how to use the questions in resolving conflicts.

Do you remember the card trick where the magician asked a series of questions to lead the volunteer to the four of diamonds? In that example, he had a finite set of numbers to choose from, so the questions were obvious. When dealing with people and relationships, however, we need more diverse and somewhat repetitive questions. This chapter examines the questions you can use and explains why they work. This is a very important chapter because, when using the ZG method, positive relationship change happens when you ask the right questions.

All of the questions are designed to help people think about their relationships in different ways. In the process of answering the questions, you and others are led to new insights and discover your own solutions. This chapter contains a comprehensive review of all the questions that are beneficial when using the ZG method. Don't worry; you will not have to use every one. In Chapters 7 and 8, I will detail how you can pick and choose which questions to use.

For ease of use, the questions have been broken into categories, following a natural progression, as follows: scaling questions, miracle questions, and other questions.

Scaling Questions

Scaling questions are used to determine the progress that people are making toward finding solutions to their difficulties. These self-indicated questions ask individuals to locate where they currently are on a scale from one to ten. In this case, a one is always the worst it can be, while a ten means that it is the best or there is no problem. The questions you will use are as follows:

- On a scale of one to ten, with one being the worst it can be and ten being no problems, where is your relationship on the scale right now?

- Where on the scale would you need to be to feel satisfied in this relationship?

- How willing are you to do your part to help make your relationship better, with one being not willing to do anything and ten being willing to do almost anything?

- How confident are you that if you do your part, your relationship will be better, with one being not confident and ten being very confident?

- In connection with this relationship, how do you feel about yourself right now, with one being the worst ever and ten being the best ever?

- How do you feel about the answer to the previous question, with one being feeling really bad and ten being feeling really good?

Most people can easily answer these types of questions. Often, they will say they are between two numbers, for example, a six and a half, which shows that they know exactly where they are on the scale. When measuring personal and relational change, a self-scoring scale is the best way to proceed. As things get better (or worse) according to the scales, change is inevitably happening.

The first scaling question, "Where is your relationship on the scale right now?" is designed to find out how severely the conflicts affect the relationship and can be reworded to fit any situation. When I am consulting with a company, I use the following: "On a scale from one to ten, with one being the worst ever and ten being the best ever, how well is your company being run right now?" This question isn't asked to get a definitive answer, but rather is used as a benchmark for further comparison. For example, one person's six may be equivalent to another person's four, but they both will know things are getting better if their numbers rise.

The second question, "Where on the scale would you need to be to feel satisfied in this relationship?" sets a goal. Some people would be satisfied if their marriage was an eight, for example, while some company managers would want their company to be running at a nine to be satisfied. This question sets a target and also establishes the improvement needed to attain that goal. So if the marriage relationship is a four and the person would be satisfied at an eight, then it needs to go up four points.

Setting these first two benchmarks is critical to the change process. For one thing, it quantifies a feeling, so it seems more real. Probably the most important result is that it makes the goal seem attainable. You might feel that your problems are so large, complicated, and entrenched that solutions are impossible. This is especially true when you have been thinking and talking about them extensively. These scaling questions, however, can offer hope when you or your relationship counterpart sees that you are only a few points away from being satisfied. It makes success seem attainable and plants the idea that maybe you can do this.

The third question, "How willing are you to do your part to help make your relationship better?" is about responsibility. Most people will answer at least a five or above on this question, because the person answering the question doesn't want to be perceived as the one who refuses to do his part to help the situation. This is a very empowering question in that it assumes that the person has a part in finding the solution.

When married couples or families are asked this question, it implies that since everyone has a part to play, then everyone is somehow responsible for the conflicts that are present. This keeps people from identifying one person as "the problem" and dispels the notion that if he or she would just change, then "we" wouldn't have any problem.

Even if the answer to this question is that they are a one (meaning not willing to do anything), it is still a helpful question. The purpose of these questions is to promote thinking and, more specifically, thinking about change. In this case, what usually happens to people who answer "one" is that later they feel very guilty about saying they wouldn't do their part and try to overcompensate by doing more than their part. So, in effect this becomes a can't-lose question that helps bring about change no matter what the answer.

The fourth question, "How confident are you that if you do your part, your relationship will be better?" asks how much ownership the person has in the problem or difficulty. Any answer of five or higher shows that the person feels a strong ownership of the problem. It is not unusual for people to put themselves at a one in reply to this question, meaning that they feel helpless to do anything about their conflicted relationship and that it is someone else's fault. Sometimes, people feel that they are a one because they have tried in the past to help make things better and nothing happened.

Often a low score will cause the person to rethink ownership of the problem and to realize that there are some things he can do that will affect the outcome. In this case, the effect is similar to the previous question, in that it is also a no-lose situation.

In marriage counseling, it isn't uncommon for one person to start out low on this scale and gradually move up as the question is asked on subsequent visits. This movement indicates that as things get better, people are more willing to show ownership in the solution than they did in the conflicts. The better things get, the more willing people are to think that they have an influence over the outcome.

In a family or business setting, as might be expected, the answers to this question will usually reflect the relative hierarchy in the group, with the more powerful individuals scoring higher and less powerful scoring lower. When working with groups, the results of these individual answers are combined, averaged, and presented to the group. When a person who has answered at the low end of the scale sees that the average is much higher, the tendency is for him to rethink his capacity to make a difference.

The fifth question, "In connection with this relationship, how do you feel about yourself right now?" is scaled as a one for the worst you have ever felt and a ten for the best you have ever felt. This question gives a measure of the person's self-image in relation to the relationship.

The sixth and final scaling question, "How do you feel about the answer to the previous question?" is scaled as a one for feel really bad to a ten for feel really good. For some individuals, this question is confusing and can be explained by asking, for example, "Do you feel like a two (pretty bad) about being a five or do you feel more like an eight (pretty good) about being a five?"

The answer to this question denotes the person's self-esteem or how that person feels about his self-image. Most importantly, this answer reveals the person's willingness to change. If an individual is a two about being a five, the person doesn't like being a five and is willing to change to move higher on the scale. However, if a person is a nine about being a five, he is fairly content where he is and doesn't have a lot of motivation for change.

These six sample questions, along with some follow-up questions detailed next, set the stage for change to proceed. The individuals have acknowledged the severity of the problem, decided at what level they would be satisfied, and have determined how willing they are to do their part to make the situation better. They have also acknowledged their responsibility level for the problems, assigned a level to their current self-image, and indicated how willing they are to change their self-image. Each of these six answers serves as a benchmark for further scaling responses. People like to watch themselves finding solutions and getting better, and these questions let them do that.

Milking the Scaling Questions

As the scaling questions are asked and answered, there are opportunities to clarify the answers with some follow-up questions. These questions can be used as needed and serve mainly as an enhancement to what has already been answered. They relate primarily to the first scaling question (Where is your relationship on the scale right now?) and the fifth scaling question (How do you feel about yourself right now?). The following types of questions can help to develop positive thinking:

- Your answer on the first scaling question was a _____. What could happen to move that relationship up one half of a point to a _____?

This question focuses on important things that would raise the score up a half of a point. For the person who is a two on the scaling question, for example, it asks what could happen so the person would answer, "I am a two and a half." This question concentrates on just a few things that can make a real difference. The question is also worded to identify something that will result in a small, incremental change.

When asked this question, most people reply with something very simple. For a married couple, it might be a verbal expression of love or appreciation. In the workplace, a simple thank you from the boss might raise a person one half of a point. And a son might say that he would go up even more than the half point if Dad would not yell at the referees during his soccer game. Like these examples, most replies to this question are easy to do and very important.

Since the answers to the scaling questions are based on feelings, it is necessary to tie them into some reality. This question accomplishes that by connecting something happening to the feeling of going up one half of a point. People should list as many answers as they can think of. This is a powerful question because the person really thinks that it can happen since it is his idea and he can see how it will come about.

The next question emphasizes that ownership even more.

- What could *you* do to bring the relationship up one half of a point?

This question asks the person to commit to his own change. Responses to the question might be that the individual would start exercising again, try to be cheerful, or plan better. Regardless of what the reply is, it means something to him. Most often, the things that people will mention to raise themselves up a half a point will be actions they have either done in the past or have been thinking about doing. They will rarely answer in a nonsensical fashion or in a way that is impossible to accomplish.

The next question brings the other person in the relationship into focus.

- What can your boss/spouse/parent/co-worker/family do to bring your relationship up one half of a point?

This question makes the individual aware of what others can do to improve the relationship and helps him recognize when others actually do some of these things. It implies that other people are also responsible for finding a solution to help things get better and seeks to identify some small marginal actions instead of looking at the whole picture.

Now that some small steps have been identified, it is time to address self-esteem issues. The fifth scaling question, "In connection with this relationship, how do you feel right now?" touches on self-image. If the individual answers this question with a one, a follow-up question would be, "What keeps you from going to a zero?" or "What keeps you from going any lower?" This follow-up question helps him be aware that no matter how bad things get, he still has some strengths that prevent him from going any lower. Just this realization alone can help him change because he sees that he has some control over how he feels.

Many times a person will respond to a scaling question with an answer that is off the scale. If it is high on the positive side, for example a twelve or a fifteen, the response might be to acknowledge the score by saying, "Oh, that would make a real difference to you." If it is low, on the negative side, for example a zero or a minus ten, the proper response would be to pick a lower number and ask, "What keeps you from going to a minus one, or to a minus twelve?" This reply reinforces the idea that no matter how low the score, the individual has some strengths that keep him from going any lower.

Another follow-up question might be "What is the highest you have ever been?" This question helps him understand that he hasn't always been this bad. Still another follow-up question might be, "Can you tell me about the time when you went up to your highest?" This question helps him realize that he hasn't always been low and that somehow, in the past, he went from a low number to a high number.

Miracle Questions

To help people change, the most important questions are future-oriented. I found the best way to talk about the future is the miracle question. This question was developed by de Shazer and Berg, and it is a terrific tool for helping people change. The question is simple: If a miracle happened tonight while you were sleeping and all the conflicts that brought you here to this point in your relationship were suddenly solved, what would be different?

Sometimes, people have trouble answering this question at first, because their difficulties seem so overwhelming that they can't imagine life without them. With a little prompting, however, most people can envision what a day would be like without their problems.

This "perfect miracle day" must be described in great detail, especially what the person is doing, seeing, hearing, and feeling throughout the day. An interesting thing happens to people as they answer this question. As my clients described their perfect day, their whole face softened, their voice became more animated, and they tended to inject humor into their story. They started to relax when they told about what their spouse, children, boss, or co-workers would be doing on this perfect day.

I must admit that the first time I used this question, I felt very apprehensive. This feeling quickly changed, however, when I saw what amazing changes came about.

It is interesting that when people answer this question, they quickly move past "I would win the lottery" or something in a similar vein. Much of what they describe has happened before, sometimes even in the recent past. In effect, what happens is the people are giving solutions to their conflicts. They know what will work to help make things better. They also remember how they described their miracle day because it is their story, and these are their solutions. This association between the perfect day and what people can do to help it come about is what brings about the change.

In describing their miracle day, people set out a blueprint of what they want to see happen. They realize their part in making it happen and start to change on their own with no prodding from anyone else. The miracle question with proper follow-up can help people change in a very short time.

Milking the Miracle Question

The miracle question is a valuable tool that lends itself to further examination. After the miracle has been described, it is important in subsequent conversations to go back and "milk" that question for more insights. These milking questions help to plot progress in finding solutions, because little by little, some of the things that have been said in response to the miracle question are already occurring. Moreover, these questions help people really believe that their miracle is going to happen, and let them see that it is coming about. Even though the changes are small, they are happening, and this gives people hope for the future. The following questions are used to enhance the miracle question:

- Are any parts of the miracle happening now? If so, which ones?

Some of the things people have said in response to the miracle question are already occurring and have, at times, happened in the previous few days. Some people may have trouble remembering all the things they said in answer to the miracle question, but as they review their response, invariably they will find things that are happening now. This question brings the miracle happening into reality. Even more concretely, if parts of the miracle are happening, it gives people hope that all of it can happen.

- What could you do to help bring this miracle day about?

This question helps people think about and understand that they can do something to help the miracle day come about, thus giving them some ownership in the process. This miracle is due in part to their own efforts.

If a person is feeling very depressed or unempowered, they may have trouble answering this question, but attempting to answer it is important. You can always go to the next question and come back to this one later.

- What are you doing now to help bring this miracle about?

This question is a follow-up to the previous one. Most of the time, people are doing things to help solve their conflicts. By recognizing this, it gives them hope that they can do even more to help the situation. Responses such as "I'm thinking about it" or "I'm talking to you" seem to help people feel more proactive. Since it is best to get the maximum number of responses from each question, it is important to list as many things as the individual can think of.

- What could your boss/spouse/parent/co-worker/family do to help bring this miracle about?

This question helps people understand that the problem is not all one person's fault and that the solution must be a cooperative effort. If this is going to be a successful solution, then everyone must be willing to change. If the person asking the question happens to be the spouse, boss, or parent, it can be helpful to rephrase the question as, "What could I do to help bring this miracle about?"

In certain instances, this question can be asked in two or more parts to indicate what specific persons could do to help bring this miracle about. In a family situation, you can ask, "What could your dad do?" "What could your mother do?" "What could your sister do?" and so on. In an organizational situation, the question could be divided into "What could your boss do?" and "What could your co-workers do?"

The next question is a follow-up to the previous one.

- Has your boss/spouse/parent/co-worker/family recently done any of the things you listed to help bring this miracle about?

This question raises the possibility that another person is already doing some of the things necessary to help bring the miracle about. It is usually the case that, whether intentionally or not, people in the situation are doing things to try to help solve it. The response to this question can be a very positive experience for both the person answering the question and for anyone else in the group. Often, there is a realization that other people are really doing something about the situation, which implies a certain amount of acknowledgment of the difficulty and a commitment to a solution.

Sometimes, other people have been doing things all along to help make things better, but they haven't been recognized because of the overwhelming nature of the conflict. This question, asked in a non-adversarial setting, can identify those things, however small, that others are actually doing. When people discover that parts of the miracle are already happening, it gives them great hope because they realize that they are already on the way to finding solutions to their conflicts.

Using the ZG method improves upon the traditional way of solving problems, where the problem is first identified and then the solution is implemented. Even if the problem can be identified, implementing the solution can cause great resistance when using the old method. Many times, people never get beyond the "How are we going to do this?" and "When are we going to start?" phases. It is like arguing about the shape of the table before sitting down to negotiate, in that it sets a tone of uncertainty, confrontation, and ill will even before the process has started.

With the ZG method, however, the individual has already started changing, and some progress has been made. The amount of progress is irrelevant, because any progress means that the process has started. When people realize that this process has already started, it removes the barrier of starting and focuses on just keeping the process going.

If the preceding question has generated little response, it can be asked in another way:

- Has your boss/spouse/parent/co-worker/family *ever* done any of the things you listed to help bring this miracle about?

Many times, several people have done some things in the past to help bring the miracle about, but they aren't doing them now. This is especially true for married couples. They often recall times when they were first married and both of them were doing things they listed as being part of their miracle day. Just saying and hearing these memories takes them back to a happier time, when their situation was better.

I have used a married couple as an example of how this question can affect a relationship, but it can also be used in a work or family setting. Most long-term relationships have had times when things were better. Recalling times when things were better at the workplace, for example, can precipitate change that re-creates a better time. Sometimes just stating that "things were better when we had lunch together" can help to bring people back to a behavior that was conducive to finding solutions.

These last three questions have been phrased to identify some small actions that will have a ripple effect on accomplishing the whole. Accomplishing small steps leads to more confidence and a belief that the whole miracle will come about. Even a small, incremental movement on the "problem" scale makes the difficulties seem a little smaller and easier to manage.

Other Questions

Visualization Questions

This set of questions is designed to help form images, sounds, and feelings that will be present when the solutions have been found and relationships are as good as they can get. This visualization exercise is similar to what many sports professionals employ before a big game. For example, while waiting on the sidelines, the field goal kicker will imagine the ball splitting the uprights, the crowd roaring, and the feeling of satisfaction as a way of programming himself for a successful kick. This same technique can be adopted to improve relationships. Imagining the better relationship helps to reinforce that it can happen, it will happen, and this is what is going to be occurring when it does happen. These questions help bring the future into focus:

- If suddenly your spouse/boss/child turned into the perfect spouse/boss/child, [pause] in what ways would you change?

When asking this question, it is important to pause where indicated. This pause provides a chance to visualize the transformation. Often during my counseling sessions, the client would say, "It would take a huge miracle to turn my boss into the perfect boss." After hearing the rest of the question, the person would say, "Oh, how would *I* change?" After he had made the mental adjustment to how he would change, he would usually reply, "I guess I would have to be perfect, too." In the reply to all of these questions, it is necessary to identify very specific actions that would occur. The following example is typical of how I helped a person give specific, concrete answers to the question "If suddenly your wife turned into the perfect wife, in what ways would you change?"

Z: How would you change?

Client: I would have to be perfect, too.

Z: What would it look like if you were perfect?

Client: I would be more cheerful.

Z: When would this occur?

Client: Mainly in the morning, when I am usually grumpy.

Z: If your wife looked at you in the morning, how could she tell you were more cheerful?

Client: She could just tell.

Z: What could you do so she would know you were more
   cheerful?

Client: I guess I could say it is a great day and give her a
   kiss.

Z: If you did that, what would she do?

Client: She would probably faint.

Z: If she didn't faint, what would she say?

Client: She would probably say, "It is a great day."

This discussion was helpful to the change process because it implied that he would change if his wife changed first. It also presented the underlying question, which is, "If you changed first and turned into the perfect husband, how would your wife change?" By not asking this question, it is left to the individual to discover on his own. Once an individual makes the connection that maybe he should go first, he is more likely to make the first move to change.

The next three questions ask about how the changes will look, sound, and feel:

- What will your marriage/workplace/relationship look like when it is the best it can be?

This question is somewhat similar, but it is meant to address people who are particularly visual in their ways of communicating. It could also be asked as, "If you were a fly on the wall, what would you see—what would people be doing?"

- What will your marriage/workplace/relationship sound like when it is the best it can be?

If the relationship is more verbal, this question might be more meaningful. An individual can describe the conversations that are taking place, or maybe the perfect workplace might be quieter, for example.

- How will you feel different when your marriage/
  workplace/relationship is the best it can be?

For people who judge how severe problems are by how they feel, this question can help put the situation into perspective. Other follow-up questions might be "What would be happening to make you feel that way?" or "How would you be feeling on your way to work?"

The purpose in answering the above questions is to draw a clear mental picture that is detailed in sights, sounds, and feelings. Visualizing the relationship in the future is a powerful tool for eliminating the negative thoughts that plague the past.

<u>Substance-Abuse Treatment Questions</u>

The next three questions come from substance-abuse counseling, but can be helpful especially when the relationship has been intensely dysfunctional for a long period of time. An addiction is simply an attempt by people to change how they feel. The key to overcoming an addiction is helping people feel better without the substance they are abusing. For substance abusers, changing other things about their addiction is often harder than the physical addiction itself. To recover, they have to change their friends, their hangouts, their habits, and the way they think. Filling all the time they spend on their addiction or thinking about it is also a major challenge.

In many ways, a conflicted relationship is like an addiction. People can't stop thinking about how terrible things are and how helpless they think they are to change it. Most people who are substance abusers spend incredible amounts of time doing or thinking about their addiction. One of the ways to assist people out of their addiction is to help them use this time in more productive ways. A tool I used to help people resolve conflicts was helping them consciously choose how to fill their time when the conflicts or difficulties were resolved. These questions address a future with less time consumed by worry, distress, and depression.

- If the conflicts in your relationship were suddenly resolved, what would you do with all the time you have been spending worrying about or trying to fix the situation? Describe what you would do instead.

This question reaffirms that the problem will be resolved and things will be different. However, if an individual persists in dwelling on, dissecting, and talking about "the problem," it will reappear and be as large as or larger than ever. It is a truism that if you look for problems, you will find them. And it is also true that no matter what has changed, if you desire to hold on to a problem, it will never go away.

Describing how the freed time will be used helps a person move away from the difficulty and toward a more life-affirming activity. It is very helpful to describe the different thought patterns that will be present when the conflicts are resolved.

For example, instead of worrying about a spouse drinking and driving, the thought pattern could be one of trust and confidence that he will do the right thing. This pattern is highly individualistic and can range from a person praying more to taking up knitting, for example.

Changing patterns of thought helps break old habits. Recovering alcoholics will usually say they imagine themselves relapsing before they actually do it. When they imagine themselves driving to the bar they pass on their way home from work, it is time to change their route home. Likewise, changing thinking patterns from problem-based to solution-based will help problems go away or greatly diminish their severity.

- When your relationship is happier, what will you be able to do that you aren't doing now?

This question prepares people for the change when it happens. Notice it asks when, not if. This change is expected and also invited. When it happens, there will be a freedom to do new and different things. Talking about these things helps the change happen.

Many times, these new things have been in a person's mind for years, but the thoughts have been discarded or put on hold because they have seemed impossible. Sometimes, these are the dreams that have kept them going through hard times, and suddenly these dreams become possible. At other times, what a person will be able to do differently is something simple but very important, like sleep or smile. Other responses might be "I could be myself" or "I could say what I am thinking without being afraid."

Poor relationships often stand in the way of people becoming who they want to be. When the relationship improves, it is no longer an impediment to people achieving their goals and objectives. This helps individuals realize that their dreams are attainable and helps the change process move faster.

- What, if anything, might present a challenge to your taking steps to improve your relationships this week? How will you meet the challenge?

This question addresses the reality that changing is not easy and there are powerful forces at work to maintain the status quo. By actively expressing a plan to overcome these challenges, new behaviors can be adopted and adverse reactions can be anticipated and defused.

Identifying the challenges allows an individual to create a plan of action in some detail for anticipated occurrences. With adequate preparation, a pending confrontation or an uncomfortable verbal exchange can be restructured to result in a more favorable outcome. Many times, these challenges are daily occurrences that keep people from changing. If this is the case, a new reaction will sometimes be enough to change the situation. It really doesn't matter what is done differently, as long as something is done that is out of the ordinary.

I once had a client who mentioned that whenever she was riding in the car with her husband, he would get angry with the other drivers and work himself into a road rage. This would lead to arguments between them and ruin their trip. To remedy this, she would try to point out other drivers' (supposed) bad habits so he wouldn't take their rude actions personally. She would say things like, "Watch out for this guy. I think he is on drugs," or "I think that woman is talking on her cell phone and playing with her dog while driving." Since she was able to convince her husband that all the other drivers were impaired in some way, he didn't take their bad driving personally anymore.

Another example of a new reaction changing the situation might be to simply give the bully a present. The playground or workplace bully might turn out to be your best friend.

As in most reactive situations, planning and change can help to diminish or extinguish behavior on the part of others that is deemed offensive. The key is to try different approaches until one works and then make it a habitual response until the problem becomes manageable or ceases to exist.

Exception Question

- Describe a time in the past when your relationship was really great. What was different?

This question looks for the exception. When problems abound and it seems as though they are long-standing, it may feel like that there haven't been any good times. This comes from the natural tendency of people to color their past with how they feel right now.

In order to dispel this type of thinking, it is necessary for the person to actively think about better times. Even when the person replies that the relationship hasn't ever been great, it is still useful to describe what was different when it was just a little better. The more detailed this description is, the more effect it will have on helping the person realize that things haven't always been this bad.

In comparing the differences between then and now, it is important to describe all the players in the relationship. Even though the thought that "I can't change someone else" might be present, it is still very important to accurately relate the situation. Relationships are interactive systems, and what one person says, does, and feels greatly affects what the others say, do, and feel.

Another important aspect to this question is to look for what was actively happening rather than what was not happening. When a person states what they don't want to happen, it just negates one possibility, but leaves all others open. For example, if a man says, "Things were really great when she wasn't nagging me," it is important to think about what she was doing instead. With more specific questions, it can be determined that she was listening and saying supportive things to him. For example, he might recall her saying, "I trust you" or "It is going to be okay" or "I know you will get it done when you have time."

This line of questioning reawakens better times and helps the person understand that this better situation can be re-created. It also helps people relearn what they already know and apply it toward changing relationships. This question is an exception because it asks the person about the past. As was discussed in Chapter 4, the ZG method is focused on future events. The only exception to this is when you ask questions about a happier time in the past.

Additional Questions

Here are some additional questions that may be helpful to think about as you work to change your relationship.

- How would you know that your relationship has started to improve even a little bit?

This question helps to make you aware of small things that might already be happening that signal an improvement. When relationships aren't going well, the tendency is to view all interactions in a negative light. Most always, positive things are happening, but are not recognized as such because of the pervasive negative attitude. When you are able to articulate the signs that would be present when improvement happens, you will be more inclined to notice these indicators and even look for them.

By looking for these signs, people will find them, and when they find them, it will be an indication that the other person is willing to repair the relationship. In answering this question, my clients would mention very small things that might happen in the normal course of the day. Some responses: "She would say good morning" or "He would kiss me" or "He would offer to help me." It is a situation where the small things mean the most.

Answers to this question were very seldom extraordinary measures, like "He would take me on a cruise," but instead focused on small, easily accomplished expressions or actions. Many times, people just wanted the other person to do some of the things they did in the past. They would say, "The old Jeff used to smile more," or "I wish Cindy would come out and play in the yard with me and the kids like she did a few years ago." It wasn't a desire to return to a time in the past; it was just a wish that the other person would exhibit some of the traits they had back then.

- As far as this relationship is concerned, what would you like to see happen now?

This question is similar to the miracle question, but it has more immediacy because it asks about now. When people change, they want to see results right away. Imagining what would happen next lets them know that the process is working and gives them confidence that it will continue to work and their miracle will be fully realized.

This question also helps you prioritize your miracle answer as to what needs to happen first so you can get maximum relief from your relational difficulties. What people want to happen now may be something they can do, or it may be something someone else has to change, or maybe both. At the very least, it prioritizes what to look for first and starts a timeline for when the miracle will finally become complete. As with the other questions, people will usually respond to this question with something that has already occurred in the past and is achievable.

- What can you do to bring out the best in your spouse/ boss/child?

Bringing out the best in people is hard work. It involves changing your point of view to see the positives in the midst of a sea of negatives. Answering this question helps to see other people in a way that accentuates their positive attributes and minimizes the negatives. It invites people to think of things that they can do to bring out the other person's best attributes.

Summary

Good questions are extremely important to the change process. Asked properly, they can help eliminate resistance to change. The main objective of all the questions in the ZG method is for you to think deeply about the solutions and to picture in your mind what it will look like when the problems are solved. Asking questions helps you do this, but the questions cannot be controlling or adversarial. In fact, probably the biggest resistance to change comes when someone more powerful suggests or insists on it.

For this reason, controlling questions should never be used. Some examples of these are as follows:

- Do you know who is in charge here?
- How can I help you change your mind?
- Why do you want to do it that way?
- Have you thought about it?
- What were you thinking about?
- Could you just try it this way?
- Are you going to do that again?
- Do I have to ask you again?
- Can you just listen for a minute?
- Why did you do that?
- Don't you see what is happening here?

Many times people use these types of questions, thinking that they are helping change come about, when in reality the effect is just the opposite. This scenario is played out millions of times each day in homes and offices, and the result is more resistance in the long run. In the short run, a person may change because the punishment or incentive is too great, but in the long run it will be self-defeating and only result in more conflict.

When asking questions to help promote change, it is important to help the person realize that no matter how bad his problems seem, he is doing some things right. Good questions help the person see a relationship in a new light.

CHAPTER 7:

HOW TO USE THE ZG METHOD AT HOME TO RESOLVE CONFLICTS

When your relationship has deteriorated to a level you can no longer accept, you can make an active decision to try to improve the situation. For some people, that means calling a counselor. Others might be unable to utilize a counselor for a variety of reasons—financial, the distance to an office, privacy concerns, or even that the other person won't go. Using the principles outlined in this book, you can get things back on track on your own. Part of the ZG method is a defined structure of questions and answers that help positive changes come about. It works like the card trick described in Chapter 4. If you don't ask the right questions, you won't get to the right card. You're not trying to identify the problem. You're looking for the solution—your "card."

When using the ZG method you conduct a series of short question-and-answer sessions spread out over three to five weeks. Each session can last from five to twenty minutes, a week apart. These sessions are more about really listening to the other person than about talking. During these sessions, specific questions are asked about future events, with no past feelings discussed. Maintaining the structure is important because it keeps the conversation concrete, positive, and in the future, eliminating the potential for hurt feelings, blame, and miscommunication.

This is a disciplined approach, and it doesn't lead to extended conversation or random thoughts. It simply consists of direct answers to direct questions. The experience is, however, very nonthreatening, and people generally report a hopeful, positive experience. Most importantly, it can produce rapid change in your relationship if you trust in the process and let it work.

The following ten steps will lead you through the process of applying the ZG method to your particular relationship situation.

STEP ONE: GET READY

It is most important to prepare yourself emotionally before initiating your first exchange using the ZG method. You must be open to change in yourself and others, and must be committed to the process. This may be the first time in quite a while that you will be able to talk to the other person about important things without having an argument.

Part of getting ready is to accept that, at least initially, you will be doing more than your half in this relationship to get it back on track. This will require you to make your changes first and to listen to some things you might not want to hear. As the initiator, you have control over the questions you ask, but you have no control over the answers.

In the exchange, you might hear hurtful things, untruths, and half-truths. The other person might also show a lack of understanding, an unwillingness to continue the conversation, or a petty meanness. You might hear things you disagree with, but this is not the time to correct the person, explain your side, or fight back. This is a time to just ask questions and listen fully and intently. If *you* are a good listener, it is more likely that the other person will just listen when it is your turn to talk.

As the initiator, you direct the conversation, and you must follow the script to get to the solution. This takes a great deal of discipline on your part. You cannot make any comment on the answers given—even if they are incorrect, frivolous, attempts at humor, or meant to push your buttons. Any deviation into a discussion about past feelings will lead to another argument and doom the effort. Be prepared to deflect questions and statements in an appropriate way, such as, "If we can get back to that later, I have a few more questions to ask," or "Can you hold that thought, and we can talk about it later?" While you are listening, you can acknowledge the answers with a nod or by saying "Okay" to show that you really are hearing what they are saying. When it is your turn to talk, an appropriate lead-in would be, "I would appreciate you just listening for a few minutes while I tell you about my miracle day."

The freedom that comes with initiating the conversation is that you don't have to do any of the things the person suggests. Your goal is to continue asking questions until you hear a suggestion that you are willing to do. It might be something you did in the past that you can start doing again or something new that you don't mind trying. Without letting your body language or facial expressions convey disapproval, you can choose to ignore any of the suggestions you hear. The miracle question may bring out some difficult responses to hear, so be ready to redirect. Answers like "You would be dead," "We would be divorced," or "You would just disappear" can be followed with, "Let's say I wasn't really dead and awakened as the perfect husband," "Let's say I turned into the perfect wife and we were remarried," or "Let's say I reappeared as the perfect parent." These responses take the conversation back to the solution instead of off the track. If the conversation starts to disintegrate into an argument or heated discussion, simply stop the process immediately by saying, "I think I would rather continue this conversation at a later date." You can always try again later.

The first few times you initiate a conversation using the ZG method, try for shorter rather than longer. Twenty minutes is ideal, but ten will work. Don't make the mistake of going too long (over forty minutes) just because it seems to be working well.

STEP TWO: DO YOUR HOMEWORK

This is probably the most important step because you are learning how to communicate in a totally different way. To understand how the ZG method works, you need to try it on yourself first. This homework process will take at least one week to accomplish before engaging in a question-and-answer session with someone else. In the first few days, you will answer the questions yourself, and during the remainder of the week, you will put some of your answers into action. Remember, it is up to you to change first, but you can do it—you have already started changing because you are reading this book.

To begin your homework, read and answer the scaling questions in Appendix I. It will be helpful if you make out a scaling question answer sheet similar to the one in Appendix II, labeled "Sample Answer Sheet for You," so you can track your answers over time and see if your relationship is improving. Next, ask yourself the miracle question (If a miracle happened and all the conflicts in your relationship were suddenly solved, what would be different?), and write down your miracle day. You can do this in outline form, paying special attention to your interactions with the person with whom you want to improve your relationship.

A typical miracle day log would be as follows:

- I get up when the alarm goes off and do not hit the snooze button.
- I smell coffee.
- Jim is already up.
- I hear quiet voices in the kitchen.
- It Sounds like Jim has the kids up and is getting breakfast.
- I take a quick shower and get dressed.
- I go to kitchen and say, "Good morning, everybody."
- Jim says, "Good morning, honey. How did you sleep?"
- I say, "Great. Better than I have slept in ages."
- I see a bowl of oatmeal and coffee at my place.
- The children are almost finished with breakfast.
- Jim goes back upstairs and gets dressed.
- I review schedules with children.
- The children get ready for school, and I compliment them on having their homework finished.
- Jim comes down, kisses me goodbye, and takes the kids to school.
- I finish breakfast, go back to the bedroom to make the bed, and it is already made.
- I go to work, etc.

Next ask yourself the question, "What could I do to help myself go up half a point on the first scaling question (How would you rate your relationship now?)?" As before, write down the answers in outline form. The example continues as follows:

- Be more patient with the kids when they forget things
- Be on time
- Talk in a quieter voice, no yelling
- Spend more time with children

- Smile more
- Dress better for work
- Be positive, especially at work

For the remainder of the week, try to do some of the things from your miracle day and one or two things from the half-point list. In our example, she would not hit the snooze button, but she would say "Good morning" to everyone and review schedules with the children from the miracle day list, and be more patient and smile more from the half-point list.

If you have more time, pick out another question or two from the list in Appendix III and list your answers as you did on the other questions. As you review these questions, notice what they have in common. They are positive, future-oriented, and concrete, and they focus on strengths. Most importantly, they are leading you to the solutions rather than asking why.

After you have answered the preceding questions for yourself and have decided which of the things you are going to do the remainder of the week, it is time to visit with Bob and Sue in Appendix IV. This example represents a typical exchange between a married couple using the ZG method.

As the initiator, Sue does her homework as previously described and simply starts the conversation. Notice how Sue leads the whole conversation, doesn't respond to Bob's answers except to clarify, and ignores attempts at starting a discussion. She also keeps asking questions until Bob can't think of anything else by saying, "Keep going," "Tell me more," and "What else?" When he is describing his miracle day, she pulls him back to the subject of their relationship by asking, "How else would we interact during the day?" Sue notes things on the miracle day that are the same on any other day and constantly shifts the conversation from negative to positive. When Bob says, "You wouldn't be in a bad mood on my miracle day," Sue replies, "If I was in a really good mood, how could you tell?"

When Bob says, "You wouldn't be complaining about my mother," Sue responds with, "Instead of complaining, what would I be saying about your mother?"

Sue constantly ignores or rephrases the negative and amplifies the positive. On the "What is better?" question, Sue ignores the "What is worse?" answers and asks for clarification on the answers that are better.

If Bob says, "You would be nicer," Sue responds, "Okay, if that happened, how would you know? What would I be saying or doing differently so you would know that I was nicer?" As the initiator, Sue is prepared to ignore "win the lottery" answers and is ready to respond to relationship-ending answers with the comment, "If I wasn't gone, but had changed into the perfect wife, what would it be like? What would happen?"

Notice how Bob's miracle day ends with him happily thinking about the peaceful day just before he goes to sleep. It is of paramount importance that the person describing the perfect day makes the connection between the actions and the results on his own. Through the answers to the questions, the respondent makes a leap of understanding and self-discovery.

Just as our card-trick magician led the volunteer to the four of diamonds through a series of questions, Sue is leading both of them to their perfect solution, which is to have a perfect ten relationship. Sue can be confident during the entire conversation because she has done her homework. She knows that if it goes badly, she can ask another question or simply end the conversation.

STEP THREE: SET THE STAGE

After you have done your homework, it is time to think about how you will initiate a conversation using the ZG method. While you were doing your homework last week, you were already setting the stage because you started to change yourself, and undoubtedly your relationship partner has noticed. Positive changes in actions and attitudes do more than anything else to start the process off on a positive note.

Another way to start the process positively is to avoid lead-in statements that trigger resistance in the other person or put their guard up before you get started. You want the other person to listen to your questions, rather than to think about being in trouble or getting chewed out. Therefore, it is imperative to avoid the following types of statements:

- We have to talk.
- I want to talk about our relationship.
- I haven't been feeling good about our relationship.
- We need to fix our marriage.
- I am not happy.
- I have some suggestions about how you can be a better partner.
- Let's have a discussion about our relationship.
- I have some questions for you.
- I just read this book that might be helpful in fixing our marriage.

Also, it is not a good idea to start this conversation in the midst of a crisis. Let the situation simmer down first. For best results, approach the person casually in an environment that is private, without distractions, and a bit spontaneous. Don't try to make this a special time in different surroundings. Just work it into everyday life. The conversation needs to feel natural. In getting started, the secret is to just start with no lead-in.

Sometimes, it is easier to start with the miracle question and miracle day. You can start as follows: "Honey, if a miracle happened tonight while we were asleep and, as a result of this miracle, our relationship was suddenly a ten or perfect, what would be different when you woke up in the morning? What would we be saying differently, doing differently, hearing differently, or feeling differently? Can you describe this miracle day?" After hearing about the miracle day, you can share your miracle day and then proceed to the scaling questions.

STEP FOUR: ASK THE QUESTIONS

In this first conversation using the ZG method, it is best to ask the six scaling questions and the miracle question. This should take twenty to thirty minutes. If after forty minutes, the conversation is going well but still not finished, simply end it until the following week. Going over forty minutes generates too much information and becomes very tiring.

While the answers are given, you can take brief notes, but if jotting notes becomes a distraction, do it later. These notes can be used for future reference and also show the person that what they have said is important to you. You shouldn't be constantly writing, but making eye contact, observing the body language, and really listening.

During this first conversation, you will record the answers to the scaling questions as in Appendix II and outline your partner's answers to the miracle day. It is important not to interrupt while the other person answers all the scaling questions and describes the entire miracle day. You can ask further questions to clarify answers or rephrase in the positive, but no other comments should be made. The results should be similar to the first session between Bob and Sue in Appendix IV.

When the other person is describing his miracle day, be especially attentive to things you could do to help his miracle day happen. During the miracle day description, you can ask, "What else would I be doing differently?" or "Can you explain a little more what would be different?" Keep asking, "What else would be different about the miracle day?" until he can't think of any more suggestions. During this miracle day conversation, it is important to focus on your relationship. Don't let the other person ramble on about the weather, peace in the world, or some other unrelated topic. It is important to take note of all the suggestions the other person has about what you would be doing differently on his miracle day.

Once you have used the right questions to draw a picture of the other person's miracle day, you can ask about your own, saying, "Do you want to hear about my miracle day?" If the person says no, just let it drop. If the person says yes, you can describe the details of your miracle day, deflecting interruptions and questions until the end. Be sure to include many things, as specific as possible, that the other person would be doing on your miracle day.

Because this method is so structured, endings must be very abrupt, such as when one person leaves the room or with a total change in the conversation topic. This might sound strange, but part of the plan is to have no extraneous conversation while using the ZG method and no debriefing afterward. Simply say, "Thanks for sharing and listening," and change the subject or leave the room.

STEP FIVE: DO SOME OF THE THINGS THAT WERE MENTIONED

By doing some of the items mentioned by the other person, you show that you heard what was said and that you want to do your part in helping the relationship move up on the scale. It is important to remember that you don't have to do all of the things that were suggested. In fact, the main reason for getting as many suggestions as possible in Step Four is so you will have many to choose from. You can do only the ones you want, and you can do the easy ones first.

If, for example, your partner suggests during their miracle day that when you leave home, you would say where you are going and when you will return, you could do that all next week.

This is about doing some small things for the next week to show that you are going to do your part. Often, some suggestions are things you did in the past when the relationship was better, so it is just a matter of resuming them again. Don't try to do anything that takes over a week because it needs to be finished before the next session. As you do some of these things, it is best not to comment on them to your partner. Nor should you comment if your partner starts to do things differently. A simple thank you will suffice—but no discussion.

<u>STEP SIX: AFTER ONE WEEK, ASK MORE QUESTIONS</u>

The second session uses the following questions:
- What is better since last week?
- Ask the six scaling questions again.
- What could I do to move our relationship up a half point on the scale?
- What could you do to move our relationship up a half point on the scale?

First, answer these questions for yourself. You can use the answer sheet to record your scaling question answers. When thinking about what is better and what changes would result in a half point of improvement, write down everything you can think of, no matter how trivial the items seem. If you think anything has been worse since last week, ignore it and remain focused on the positive.

As before, your answers to the questions can be shared later in the conversation. When asking the "What is better?" question, keep probing until your partner says two or three things that are better. You aren't interested in hearing about what is worse, so ignore those comments.

With the scaling questions, it is important to record the answers and compare those answers to the ones last week. You should comment about how they are different up or down, but avoid discussions about why they are up or down. If the other person makes a comment, simply acknowledge it and move on. Write down the suggestions your partner has of things you could do to help him move up on the relationship sale.

This second conversation should be easier than the first because both of you know the routine, but don't violate the rules and go too long or start a discussion about what is happening.

STEP SEVEN: DO SOME OF THE THINGS YOUR PARTNER SUGGESTED THE FOLLOWING WEEK

As before, do the things you want to do and can do easily, and that are important to the relationship. Also, continue doing the things you were doing differently last week. This is important because you need to show your partner that this is a permanent change.

STEP EIGHT: AFTER ONE MORE WEEK, ASK MORE QUESTIONS

By now, both you and your relationship partner know the drill. Hopefully, when you ask the question "What is better?" your partner will respond with a number of things. It is also important to ask and record the scaling questions again so both of you can see the progress that has been made the last three weeks. In this third conversation, it might be helpful to select additional questions from the list in Appendix III. You can choose questions that will be most helpful in strengthening your particular relationship. As before, write down your answers prior to the conversation and volunteer to share them with your partner. Also, record suggestions your partner makes that will help the relationship.

STEP NINE: DO SOME MORE SUGGESTIONS

Keep doing the suggestions you have already adopted and try to add one or two more from this last conversation. Usually after three question sessions and three weeks total, the relationship is better. Keep having these sessions, using the ZG method, until your relationship is where you want it to be. You can tell when to stop the process because the answers to scaling questions one and two will be the same. In other words, your relationship has come up on the scale to where you are satisfied. You have reached your "card."

STEP TEN: FOLLOW UP

After you move your relationship up the scale to the point where you are satisfied, you've succeeded. In the case of a married couple, a good marriage is just a series of falling in love over and over again; there will be down times. When your relationship dips down, you just pull the book back out. It's okay. This method of communication allows for our human failings. It's the nature of life that we might fall away from the little things and fall out of rhythm. With the communication tools described in this book, you can easily use this language to repeat the exercise throughout your relationship.

OTHER FAMILY SITUATIONS

The ZG method for couples and families, as described, is most useful with people who interact daily for a period of weeks. It is ideal for married couples, engaged couples, and longtime partners living together. For other family situations, the method can be abbreviated to one or two very short sessions.

For example, if a father wanted to improve his relationship with his fourteen-year-old daughter, the conversation might go as follows:

Father: If a miracle happened and I turned into the best dad in the world for you, what would be different?

Daughter: What would be different?

Father: Yes. How would I be different? What would I be doing differently?

Daughter: Well, you would double my allowance.

Father: Okay. What else?

Daughter: You would let me go on car dates by myself.

Father: Okay. What else?

Daughter: You would extend my curfew two hours.

Father: Okay. What else?

Daughter: You would knock first instead of just barging into my room.

Father: Okay. What else?

Daughter: You would stop giving me grief about my boyfriend.

Father: Okay. What else?

Daughter: You wouldn't tease me about my weight.

Father: Okay. What else?

Daughter: That's all I can think of.

Father: Okay. Thanks.

In about two minutes, the father has learned what he can do to improve his relationship with his daughter. He is probably not going to do the first three things she suggested, but she knew that when she said them. This was just her way of baiting him to see if he was really going to listen this time. When she didn't get a negative response, she felt free to share things that were really interfering with their relationship. It was the last three things that were the most important and the easiest for the father to change. By complying with her last three suggestions, the father can greatly enhance their relationship. Using this form of the miracle question is sometimes more effective than other ways of repairing relationships because the initiator chooses what to do. There are no broken promises.

One of the keys to using the ZG method is to start small with easy questions and a very limited time frame. Even when a session is successful, keep the time frame brief. You can always expand upon those ideas at a later date. And if any session seems to be unsuccessful, try again later with different questions.

CHAPTER 8:

How to Use the ZG Method at Work to Resolve Conflicts

In today's business environment, companies and organizations have to function effectively, but many things can disturb the smooth running of an operation, including personalities, personal events, and outside events. Today, organizations face downsizing, rightsizing, buyouts, mergers, new technology, and uncertain world events. These forces, when combined with normal personnel turnover and job shifting, can result in a disruption of good relationships at work. The ZG method can be used to resolve conflicts and restore these important workplace relationships. People should care about these relationships because, generally speaking, the better their relationships, the happier they are at work. In turn, this affects their team, division, and ultimately the entire organization. In most workplaces, the key to productivity is the competence and the positive interactions of the people who work there.

Managing change in an organization is an old subject. There have been countless books and articles written about all aspects of managing and creating change in business. Usually, any attempt at change starts with something that the board, manager, or team leader misidentifies as a "problem." Consultants are called in to solve the problem. After asking lots of questions and making innumerable flip charts and PowerPoint presentations, they are ready to present their findings and final recommendations. This meeting is usually a big disappointment because nothing new comes out. Many times, the final result is that nothing really changes, and the report gets filed away. Sometimes, the recommendations set up competitive structures, where everyone is competing against one another for customers or additional business. This usually results in a lack of cooperation, less interaction, bad feelings, and more "problems."

Instead of calling outside consultants, the company manager or team leader can use the ZG method to produce real change when dealing with interpersonal relationships. When a manager recognizes an organizational conflict, a meeting can be called, and through skillful questioning, the solution becomes obvious, and because the suggestions come from the team members, they are more likely to implement the changes. The ability to adapt and change is vital to all organizations, but problems with teamwork and interpersonal relationships can get in the way. Using the ZG method gives leaders a tool to remove these roadblocks and create a positive, collaborative workplace.

STEP ONE: PROBLEM OR CONFLICT?

To effectively resolve an issue in any organization, you must first define it as a problem or a conflict. As we explored in Chapter 4, problems are concerned with things—machines, software, directives, policies, historical procedures, or anything that is not a person. To correct these problems, it is best to use the scientific method. However, if the situation involves people, it is best to use the ZG method to discover the solution. A little investigation can usually determine if the difficulty is a thing problem or a people conflict, but sometimes this distinction isn't clear. If two people are operating the same equipment on different shifts, for example, it might be hard to determine if the difficulty is with the equipment or with the individuals. Does the equipment break down because of a design malfunction, operator error, poor maintenance, or sabotage? When in doubt, start with the ZG method first. If the problem is determined to be with the machine, you can change to the scientific method to solve it. The biggest mistake is to try to resolve conflicts involving people by using the scientific method instead of the ZG method. Doing this usually results in blame, finger pointing, hurt feelings, or strained relationships and never gets to the real solution.

STEP TWO: GET READY

After you have determined that you have a conflict, you can get ready to lead your employees through the process. This structure closely resembles a counseling situation, where the counselor acts as a moderator and helps people mend relationships between themselves. Remember, like the magician, you ask the questions and draw out the solution. The solution, as always, is the answer to the question, "If our company or organization was a ten, or the best it could be, what would be different?"

You as the moderator are leading the whole process, asking questions and never giving opinions or suggestions. This approach takes discipline on your part because you, in many cases, are the manager. As I experienced as a counselor, an answer may seem obvious to you, but the solution will only be embraced if it comes from the people involved. You must listen and not make any comment about what is being said, even if the answers are incorrect or frivolous. In general, the moderator simply listens, makes a few notes, and asks the right questions to lead the person or group to the solution. You shouldn't be constantly writing, but making eye contact, observing the body language, and really listening.

Prior to using the ZG method in your organization, it is important to review Chapters 6 and 7 and read Bob and Sue's exchange in Appendix IV. This reading will give you a good overview of the ZG method and insight into the questions you can ask. The scaling questions and the miracle question will be the basis of most interactions using this method, but you can choose to use other questions if you feel they may be more appropriate.

You must be prepared for some difficult responses that will need to be redirected. Answers like "Double our pay and vacation," "Fire the boss," and "No more meetings like this one" need to be rephrased in the positive and redirected to the future after the miracle has taken place. A possible response could be, "Well, after the miracle when this company is a ten, what would you be doing that would deserve a raise? How would you be working differently?"

STEP THREE: SET THE STAGE

The mechanics of using the ZG method are very similar, whether it is used at home or in the workplace. Because the organizational setting is not as intense or emotional as in the home, the sessions can resemble a typical business meeting and can be held at regular staff meetings. It is important to set the stage and determine what type of meeting will be most effective.

When using the ZG method in a business or organization, there are four basic formats. They are as follows:

- Conversations with an individual
- Interactions with two people
- Informal small groups
- Formal large groups

The first two formats are similar to the situations encountered in Chapter 7 (How to Use the ZG Method at Home to Resolve Conflicts), and most of the same techniques apply. The main differences are that the individual initiating the conversation acts as the moderator and the conversations are shorter (five to fifteen minutes) and much less intimate.

When having a conversation with an informal group of five to twenty people, the time frame is twenty to thirty minutes. At a minimum, with this type of group, you need to meet at least four times, spaced a week or two apart. Participants should be arranged in a circle, but tables are not a necessity, as note-taking is limited.

The formal group conversation is different and begins with a questionnaire followed by two or three meetings. An example of this formal group presentation is in Appendix VI and is used when the group is too large or too geographically dispersed to come together in one location. The results of the questionnaire are averaged, compiled, and presented to the group in the first meeting.

When working with groups in both informal and formal settings, it is important to set the stage so that the amount of negative feedback is kept to a minimum. The ZG method is future-oriented and an exercise in "What if?" Any agendas or notes sent out before the meeting should reinforce this concept.

STEP FOUR: DO YOUR HOMEWORK

This is perhaps the most important step in learning the ZG method. Even though you are the moderator in all four formats and will not share your opinions, it is important that you ask yourself some of the questions first. This will help you understand how the method works and keep within the structure of resolving conflicts and not solving problems.

It is important to review the first part of Chapter 7, especially Step Two: Do Your Homework. The biggest difference between using the ZG method at home and using it at work is the use of a moderator. Also read over Bob and Sue's conversation in Appendix IV, noticing how Sue skillfully keeps the conversation positive and future-oriented.

It would be helpful if you could arrange to have a trial run, especially before you facilitate a group meeting. Conducting a practice conversation with friends or family members will enable you to get a feel for the process. During this time of preparation, try to think about how you would respond to different answers in a way that leads to the solution.

After you have done this homework, it is time to pick the questions you will ask. Be sure to read over the list of questions in Appendix V and select those that seem most appropriate to your situation. It is important to keep the time frame in mind so you don't select too many questions. When using the ZG method with one or two individuals, five to fifteen minutes is best. For larger groups, twenty to thirty minutes per session is sufficient. You can always meet again later.

Spreading the process between several short conversations has two benefits. The first is that people can't remember all the conversation if it is too long. The other is that the change happens between the conversations, so the seeds get planted and then need time to grow.

STEP FIVE: THE FIRST MEETING

When you feel confident enough as a moderator, it is time to begin the conversations and meetings. To best illustrate how the ZG method is used in the four formats, I have included some sample conversations in this section. Individual conversations do not need a written agenda or introduction; you can just go right to the pertinent questions. On the other hand, meetings with larger groups might require some notice about the meeting topic, but keep the information brief.

As the moderator, you will sometimes feel as though you wasted everyone's time and accomplished nothing. The key is to follow the process exactly and be patient. People will start to respond to their own suggestions, and you will see new attitudes start to emerge. Everyone wants to have relationships that are a ten, and they want to work for a company or organization that is a ten. With your help, they can make it happen.

Conversation with an Individual

Interactions with a single person most closely resemble using the ZG method at home as detailed in Chapter 7. Many employers offer a benefit of free personal counseling to their employees, and when I was in the counseling business, a large part of my work supported these employee assistance programs. Much of the counseling I did dealt with typical marriage and family issues, but some of it was related to how the employee felt about working for the company. When I used the ZG method in conversations with them, these people were able to see their company in a new light and become re-energized about their work life.

In the first example, the owner of a small business notices that Carol's morale is low and approaches her at the end of a break period, when she is alone.

Owner: Carol, if our company was a ten, or the best it could be, what would be different?

Carol: What do you mean?

Owner: For instance, what would be different when you came into work first thing in the morning?

Carol: Well, people would be smiling and they would say good morning.

Owner: Then what would you say?

Carol: I would probably say, "Good morning," too.

Owner: What else would be different?

Carol: I would probably be dressed up a little more.

Owner: What do you mean?

Carol: Maybe I would wear a dress or a skirt instead of just pants all the time, and I would take the time to curl my hair in the morning instead of just putting it up in a ponytail.

Owner: Was there a time in the past when you dressed up more?

Carol: Oh, yes. When I first started here three years ago, I always looked good when I came to work.

Owner: What else was different three years ago when you came to work?

Carol: I looked forward to coming to work. On the drive over, I felt glad to have my job and was excited about seeing everybody.

Owner: Is your team about the same as it was three years ago?

Carol: Yes, about the same.

Owner: Do some of your team members smile and greet you in the morning like they did in the past?

Carol: Yes, some of them do.

Owner: What could you do to help make our company the best it can be?

Carol: I guess I could be more excited about work like I was three years ago.

Owner: I enjoyed our chat. Maybe we can talk again next week.

The owner simply asks, "If our company was a ten, or the best it could be, what would be different?" Based on Carol's responses, the owner uses the exception question to see if there was a time in the past in which she did these things. Through skillful questioning using the ZG method, the owner has helped Carol connect back to a time when work was more enjoyable.

The questions also help Carol realize that the team is basically the same, and it is Carol who has changed. This conversation took just a few minutes in a very informal setting, but got Carol to think about her attitude and how she could be more positive.

Interactions with Two People

The next format involves the manager talking separately to two people who are having difficulty working together. In this example, the newly hired manager is concerned because he quickly realizes that his two assistant managers, Tom and Jim, don't get along and rarely speak to each other. The other employees told him this has been going on for about two years, but they don't know how or why it started. The manager decides to use the ZG method to try and get Tom and Jim to start communicating again. The manager asks Tom to stop by his office when he has a chance.

Manager: Thanks for coming by, Tom. Let's just say that a miracle happened in the middle of the night and the next morning you and Jim are getting along really well. In fact, let's say your relationship was a ten, or the best it could be. If this happened, how could you tell that the miracle happened when you came into the office the next day? What would be different?

Tom: Well, as I went by Jim's desk on the way to mine, I guess he would say, "Hi, Tom."

Manager: How would you respond?

Tom: You mean after the miracle?

Manager: Yes, after the miracle.

Tom: Well, I guess I would say, "Hi" back.

Manager: How would the remainder of the day go?

Tom: Well, I guess it would be like it was in the old days.

Manager: How was that?

Tom: Jim and I were good friends, and we would go to dinner with our wives and have a good time.

Manager: So in the old days, how did you and Jim interact at work?

Tom: We got along great.

This conversation is presented in an abbreviated form. In reality, it would last twenty to thirty minutes as the manager asked for more details about the miracle day, using questions from Appendix V.

Manager: Thanks for talking with me, Tom. Can we meet about the same time next week?

Tom: Sure.

In this example, the manager immediately asked the miracle question, which sets the tone. He milked the question for more details and then asked the exception question to learn more about a time when they got along. Notice how the manager never asks what went wrong or why they stopped getting along. He doesn't need to know, and it won't help the process.

The manager has a similar twenty- to thirty-minute conversation with Jim soon after meeting with Tom and gets a similar response. Answering the miracle question and talking about a time when they got along allows Tom and Jim to see the benefits of resuming a cordial relationship on their own. Better yet, they both saw that the better relationship could begin with just a simple greeting.

Informal Small Group

The informal small group setting is for up to twenty people and is designed to help the group or team function better together. In this example, the manager at a small manufacturing plant with ten workers feels negativity might be hurting productivity. He calls a team meeting to search for solutions and seats the group in a circle of chairs. This manager is well versed in the ZG method and uses it to lead the group discussion.

Manager: Thank you all for coming. This will only take about twenty minutes. I want to start with six scaling questions. Your answers will be on a scale of one to ten, with ten being the best and one being the worst. Please don't interrupt while someone else is answering or comment on any of the answers. Just answer when it's your turn and listen when it's not. The first question is: On a scale from one to ten, with one being the worst and ten being the best, how well is our company running right now? We'll start here and go around the circle. Just shout out your answer.

Group: Each person in the group shouts out answers one at a time, and the manager records them. [This is how they will answer each question.]

Manager: If my math is correct, the average of all the answers is about a four and a half. Now, how willing are you to do your part to help the company run better? A one means you aren't willing to do anything at all, and a ten means you would do almost anything. [The answers are given and averaged.] The average is about a nine. And how confident are you that if you did do your part, things would be better? A one means you aren't confident at all, and a ten means you are very confident. [The answers are given and averaged.] Okay, it seems that you are about a seven and a half on this question. How do you feel about your work right now? A one is the worst ever, and a ten is the best ever. [The answers are given and averaged.] The answers average about a six. How do you feel about your answer to the previous question? A one means you feel really bad about your answer, and a ten means you feel really good. [The answers are given and averaged.] Okay, the average here is about a four. Collectively, your answer to the first question, how well is our company being run, was a four and a half. What could happen to move it up half a point to a five?

Worker #1   One thing that would bring it up half a point would be if our machines wouldn't break down as often.

Worker #2   If that happened, it would bring it up a lot more than half a point.

Worker #3   The company would be more like a six instead of a four and a half.

Manager: What else could happen to bring our company up a half of a point?

Worker #4   We would have more help.

Worker #5   I agree. When someone was sick or on vacation, they would get a replacement instead of all of us working overtime.

Worker #6   Everything would run better if we had extra help.

Manager: What could *you* do to bring your score up a half point to a five instead of a four and a half?

Worker #7   Probably stop complaining so much.

Worker #8   We could all stop complaining.

Manager: What else could you do to bring our score up?

Worker #9   We could try to be on time more so we could get started right away.

Worker #10   Yes and we would call in if we are sick instead of just not showing up.

Manager: Thanks for your help. I see it is about five o'clock, so we will adjourn. We will meet again next week, same time and place.

In this meeting, the manager was able to establish some benchmarks using the scaling questions. In the next session, he will ask the same questions to see if the workers' opinions have moved up or down. He was also able to elicit some comments about what could happen to bring the company up and what the employees could do to help bring the company up. Plus, everyone in the group heard the responses and can start to see their role in improving the company.

Formal Large Group

The final use for the ZG method in business situations is more formal. This format is used when all of the team members can't be together at once or when a written record is desired. This format begins with each team member filling out a questionnaire with five scaling questions and fourteen other questions. The leader compiles the individual questionnaires into a single report, which is then reviewed with all the team members.

The five scaling questions are rated on a scale of one to ten, with ten being the best and one being the worst. The next fourteen questions use the miracle question and various milking questions to help create a shared vision of the future. These questions allow the participants to see how they can do their part to contribute to this vision. An example of this format can be found in Appendix VI.

STEP SIX: AFTER ONE WEEK, ASK MORE QUESTIONS

About a week after your first meeting or conversation, it is time to ask more questions. Many times, you are revisiting the scaling questions to check for movement on the scales and asking what is better since the last meeting. You can also use any questions in Appendix V you think might be appropriate.

Let's revisit some of our examples to see how the subsequent conversations play out. In the Conversation with an Individual example, Carol was lagging in morale.

Owner: Well, Carol, I haven't had a chance to talk to you for a week or so, and I was wondering if anything at work is better than it was last week.

Carol: Not really. It's pretty routine and boring.

Owner: Just think a minute. It can be anything, no matter how small. Is anything better?

Carol: Well, I got a couple compliments when I dressed up more on Tuesday.

Owner: Anything else better?

Carol: Well, I ate lunch in the break room instead of at my desk. It was nice to chat with everyone. I really like everyone here. It's a real friendly place.

Owner: Anything else better about work?

Carol: My supervisor rearranged my schedule last week so I could come in late after taking my mom to the doctor, and I really appreciated that. She always tries to accommodate people who have family issues.

Owner: Anything else better, Carol?

Carol: No, not really.

Owner: Thanks for taking the time to visit with me, Carol.

In this second meeting with Carol, the owner asks the "What is better?" question. When Carol says she can't think of anything that is better, the owner urges her to find something, no matter how small. This is an example of a brief, casual conversation designed to help Carol realize that there are some good things happening at work and that she is making small changes that are helping her enjoy work more.

The owner can continue having these conversations with Carol from week to week, never offering suggestions or answers, but continuing to lead Carol with good questions until her morale has improved. As they talk, Carol will provide her own suggestions, and because they came from her, she is more likely to try them.

In the second example, covering interactions with two people, Jim and Tom were assistant managers who didn't speak to each other despite being old friends. The manager speaks with each of them individually at first. For the second meeting, he brings them together. The manager is careful not to bring up the fact that they have hardly talked for two years.

Manager: Thanks for coming by, Tom and Jim. I'd like you to answer a few scaling questions for me. The answers will be on a scale of one to ten, with ten being the best and one being the worst. Please just listen while the other person is answering. Don't interrupt or comment on any of the answers. The first question is, on a scale from one to ten, with one being the worst and ten being the best, how would you rate your working relationship right now? Jim?

Jim: About a two.

Manager: Tom?

Tom: A three.

Manager: Now, how willing are you to do your part to improve your working relationship? One means you aren't willing at all, and ten means you would do almost anything. Tom?

Tom: I'm a nine.

Jim: Nine too.

Manager: What could happen to improve your working relationship that would maybe move your rating on the first question up just a half a point?

Jim: We could start having our weekly update meeting again.

Tom: And we could share team members if one of our projects gets backlogged.

Manager: Anything else?

Tom: We could play eighteen some Saturday.

Jim: Yeah. And maybe meet up with our wives for dinner afterwards.

Manager: I've got another meeting to run to. Thanks for talking with me.

The next week, the manager saw Tom and Jim come in together one morning, and he knew all was well. The rest of the office was amazed that after two years of not talking, suddenly Tom and Jim were conversing like old times. The only one who wasn't surprised was the new manager. He was very skilled at using the ZG method and had seen it work like that before.

With the informal small group, our manager was trying to improve productivity by reducing negativity. A week later, he pulls his staff back together for another meeting.

Manager: Good afternoon. I would like to start off by asking you the same questions as last week, the ones with a scale from one to ten, with one being the worst and ten being the best. We'll go around the room for answers just as before. Where are you on the scale for how well your company is running right now? [The answers are given and averaged.] Okay, that averages about five and a quarter, so that is three quarters of a point better than last week. The next question is how willing are you to do your part to help make things better? [The answers are given and averaged.] That average is a little over nine, so it is about the same. How confident are you that if you do your part, things will be better? [The answers are given and averaged.] That is about eight, so it is up half a point from last week. And how do you feel about your work right now? [The answers are given and averaged.] That is about six and a half, which is a half point better. And how do you feel about being a six and a half? [The answers are given and averaged.] Your answers average about five, which is up a full point from last week. Most of these are up from last week. What is better?

Worker #1 The maintenance guys have kept the machines running better.

Worker #2 And they fixed up one of the old machines we can use as a spare if necessary.

Manager: What else is better?

Worker #3 It seems like people are better at showing up for work on time.

Manager: Let's say that we had the best plant in the whole country. If that happened, what would be different about our plant?

Worker #4 There would be more cooperation.

Manager: What kind of cooperation?

Worker #5 Well, if someone got behind and someone else was finished, they would come and help the person who is behind.

Worker #6 Yes. We would be more like Abby.

Manager: What do you mean, "more like Abby"?

Worker #7 Abby always helps other people whenever she has extra time.

Worker #8 Yes, and she never complains, either.

Worker #9 I always know when Abby is eating in the lunchroom because instead of complaining, everyone is laughing and joking and having a good time.

Worker #10 If everyone was like Abby, this place would be the best. No question.

Manager: If working here was the best, what else would be different?

Worker #1 I would be looking forward to coming to work instead of sometimes dreading it.

Worker #2 Another thing that would be different is that we would always be finished on time because the equipment works and we would be helping each other.

Manager: Well, I see it is about five o'clock. Thanks for coming.

In this second meeting, the manager compares the scaling questions and finds that they have gone up. When using the scaling questions, it can be helpful to write the answers on a white board so everyone can see how they compare. He asks what is better, to amplify the reasons things are better, and he asks his employees to visualize the company at its best. Talking about what Abby does uses the exception question to illustrate what has worked in the past.

These sessions are designed to help the group believe that things are getting better and to set a goal. In these types of informal meetings, there isn't any need for notes or other written record other than the numerical answers. Each person hears what the others have said, and they remember it because they live it every day. This is a good way to promote teamwork, when the whole team can be assembled together.

In the formal large group, the second step is actually the first meeting. After the questionnaires have been collected, the moderator compiles the answers into one document to be shared with the group. This is helpful because each team member can see how the whole team feels about each question. The moderator can also summarize the results, focusing on the positive and on where the participants are open to change. A sample compiled report and summary recommendations can be found in Appendix VI. This information is a valuable tool for helping the group to arrive at workable solutions in which they have ownership.

In subsequent meetings, the scaling questions and the "What is better?" question can be asked to chart the progress of the group. Smaller teams can be formed to find solutions to the issues raised. A list of questions for team meetings is included in Appendix VII to help start the team dialogue. Using these questions will keep the process focused on the future and on finding solutions.

STEP SEVEN: FOLLOW UP

Congratulations on leading your employees or co-workers through this process! Once the desired changes have started to occur, it is important to never go back and talk about what went wrong in the past. Remain focused on the future and know that you can always revisit these questions in future conversations. It is quite beneficial to continue using the language of the ZG method in routine team meetings and staff meetings with individuals. In Appendix VII, I have included other questions that I recommended to managers and team leaders when I did leadership consulting for organizations. When reviewing these questions, you will see common threads: They are positive and future-oriented, and focus on the strengths of the individual or team.

By now, you may have noticed that many of the characteristics of the ZG method are also traits of effective leadership. Both the ZG method and good leaders focus on people and relationships first. Both the ZG method and good leaders emphasize people's strengths and potential. Both the ZG method and good leaders also have more questions than answers and are able to lead people to find their own solutions. Both share authority and empower rather than control. Both promote teamwork, self-discovery, change, and renewal. Both foster commitment in people and get them to cause change, not just support it.

In every successful organization, a key to that success is helping managers become effective leaders who promote good relationships. In general, managers are addicted to problem solving—that's what they get paid to do. Unfortunately, when they are put in a leadership position, they often try to solve relationship conflicts by finding the "problem." We have seen that this approach won't work and usually makes things worse. If these leaders use the ZG method, it will help them manage people more effectively and create positive change in their organizations.

CHAPTER 9:

MAINTAINING THE CHANGE

Persist in the Change

Sometimes change is hard, especially when you have to be willing to change *yourself*. This may happen because of some enlightenment, because of a sense of impending doom if you don't change, or maybe just because you want to.

Change can come about slowly, over a period of years, or almost instantaneously, as if you have just "seen the light." If it happens fast, it doesn't mean that people are insincere. In fact, they have probably thought about it for a very long time. Regardless of how it happens, it is often painful to stop certain behaviors and old ways of thinking and to adopt new ones. It is a process of reinventing yourself as the person you want to be. This is the person you see in your future-envisioning process.

In my counseling practice, I have seen this transformation many times. Sometimes, it is so dramatic that the client will refer to himself as the "old Tom" and the "new Tom." The client describes how the "new Tom" is going to handle things differently. Invariably, the "new person" has more energy, looks forward to the day, and has a plan and a vision for the future. The client also decides to discard many of the things that the "old person" did, such as arguing, raising his voice, losing his temper, and being too picky. Instead, the client has a new plan for what he is going to do in particular situations.

Problems arise when you are unable to accept the changes, either in yourself or in another person. This is so key in helping people change that it was explored in Chapter 5: Laying the Groundwork for Success--Be Willing to Change Yourself. When someone else changes, you must change in order to accept that new person. If this doesn't happen, the change is doomed from the beginning.

One client admitted that her husband had changed and turned into the perfect spouse, but she divorced him anyway. She couldn't accept the "new person." Interestingly, her next marriage was to a man who was doing the same things as her former husband, after the changes. She could accept the behavior from a man she hadn't known before, but not from her changed husband.

Most people judge others on their past behavior so, in a very real sense, a person's past follows him around, preventing change. This is why, for people seeking to change a relationship, they must persist in the change until a new history can be written.

When clients ask me how long it will be before others accept the change, I tell them that in one month, things will be much better, but it will take about six months before people really accept the new person.

Often, the past is a bigger obstacle than we think. When there has been a serious relationship breakdown, there are many hurt feelings because of things that were said and done. Even if the people in the relationship have changed and thus are no longer the same as when the hurt feelings occurred, the wound still festers. To some people, allowing the other person to change and move on in the relationship would be like pretending that nothing hurtful happened in the past.

It is essential not to listen to those voices of the past that attempt to sabotage the change process. Those voices can be your inner voice or the voices of other people close to you. Although the results are positive, the process of change can be difficult. When well-meaning relatives and friends see this struggle, they may want to relieve the pain and advise the person to stop the change process, usually by recommending divorce or estrangement from the other person.

My advice to the people in these situations is to not listen to this short-sighted advice, but to work through it for themselves. Without change, they often repeat the same mistakes in their next relationship. One client came in and said, "I am really worried about my marriage."

When I asked what the trouble was, he said, "My second wife is starting to act just like my first wife."

The key to overcoming the difficulty of the change process and the ghosts of the past is combating these obstacles with a more powerful motivator—a positive vision of the future. To make change come about, focus on your positive future vision and do not ever think about the past disappointments, because those thoughts will only pull you down. You must always focus on where you want to go, not where you have been. Using the principles discussed in prior chapters, you can create a vision of exactly how you want to be and imagine how you will react in every circumstance. Then just maintain this better behavior, no matter what happens, until you and others can accept the new you.

Stay Positive, Focus on the Future, and Emphasize Strengths

A good friend once told me that he wouldn't allow himself the luxury of a negative thought. He explained that just the process of engaging in negative thinking sets in motion a whole series of events that often render him incapable of being who he wants to be. Negative images of self can often follow negative thoughts to the point that the person becomes incapable of action or can only act in a negative way, starting the dreaded downward spiral.

Negative thoughts come from many sources, but probably the most harmful come from past unpleasant experiences. Maybe an individual has had a fight with his spouse, a disagreement with a co-worker, or a painful event during childhood. Thinking about and dwelling on these negative past events is very harmful in trying to overcome them. Despite the traditional approach to counseling, where clients are asked to recall every negative thing that ever happened to them, I try not to discuss these negative thoughts. This type of negative thinking is not helpful and is usually very harmful to the person. As we have seen, a past problem does not have to be identified in order to find a solution. Focusing on the past doesn't help the person change. In fact, many times it prevents change because the individual has now found a reason to stay as he is.

When a person is in the midst of change, it is very important to stay positive in all ways. This is a very vulnerable time. Negative thinking can subvert the change process and cause the person to revert to his former behavior and way of thinking. Negative thoughts like "This isn't going to work," "They can see through me," or "I can't do this" doom the change process. If people know that the change is best for them and their relationships, they must focus on the positive aspect at all times. Having a positive outlook and focusing on the future has a great effect on a person's life.

Change only happens in the future. That is why successful people spend virtually all of their time thinking about the future. They don't spend time hashing over past problems or failures but see the road ahead as more important. This is a very hopeful attitude, supported by the belief that things will be better, and they have the confidence that individual efforts will succeed. Since the future is unknown, it can be anything you want it to be. Having a definite vision of that future helps it come to fruition.

Emphasizing strengths is another important part of helping people change. People will more easily move toward an area where they feel competent and confident rather than toward weakness. It is a matter of not worrying about what you lack, but going with what you have. A good way to emphasize strengths is to point out those times when a person acted in an exemplary way. Positive people are always looking for ways to compliment others on their good behavior. For example, this can be when a mother compliments her child for sharing, or when a wife tells her husband how well he cooks on the outside grill.

Too many times a boss, spouse, or parent will try to help a person change by pointing out his weaknesses. People are already aware of their weaknesses and failures and don't need to be reminded of them. Focusing on people's weaknesses just pulls people down and frustrates them.

The key is to focus on the person's strengths and help him just to manage his weaknesses. When this happens, the strengths overwhelm the weaknesses, and the person can be successful in attaining his goals. Focusing on strengths and things that a person does well produces satisfaction, pride, a positive self-image, and success. It promotes a "can-do" attitude and leads the person toward an area where he can excel. A wonderful book about using strengths is *Soar with Your Strengths*, by Donald O. Clifton and Paula Nelson.

This section can be easily summed up: Focus on the positive, not the negative. Focus on what you can do, not on what you have done. Focus on your strengths, not your weaknesses. The success of the ZG method is rooted in having positive expectations about what will happen when you use your strengths.

Visualize the Person as Having Already Changed

How we treat people speaks very powerfully to them, to us, and to everyone else. In general, people treat others how they perceive them to be right now. The image we have of a person and how we treat that person is shaped by what we know about him, what we have heard about him, how we physically observe him, and other somewhat stereotypical traits we assign. Almost all of these traits we ascribe to the individual come from past experiences. This is such a natural action that we don't even think about how these thoughts are formed. This usually works in a satisfactory manner in daily interactions, but when trying to help a person change, it won't work effectively.

If you treat people as they are, their capacity to change is diminished because the present is reinforced in a way that prevents change in the future. However, if you treat people like they will be when their problems are solved, then they tend to fulfill that expectation you have of them. This is an act of believing in another person. Most of us have interacted with someone who really believed in us. These individuals say things like, "You will get through this" or "You are having a tough time, but when it is over you will be a better person." Parents, teachers, and grandparents seem to be good at this sort of thing. They have the ability to see beyond the current crisis and know that things will be better. The ability to see people in the future as transformed for the better helps to bring out the best in them. For example, grandparents have had the experience seeing children grow up, so they know how children turn out. In the midst of sibling rivalry, they might point out to their grandchildren that when they get older, they will be the best of friends, just like their dad and Uncle George are now.

When I started using the ZG method in counseling couples, one of the biggest differences was how I viewed the couple. Since we never talked about past conflicts, weaknesses, and fault finding, the only way I got to know the couple was through their miracle days and answers to other future-oriented questions. Basically, I saw them as a couple that had a marriage that was a ten, because that is all we talked about. Because of this, I would automatically treat them that way.

Focusing on people's strengths or their goodness also helps them to change for the better. A person who can see compassion in an otherwise unruly teenager can help that adolescent change his self-image. Noticing an act of kindness and remarking that a person has compassion for others helps make a person more compassionate.

If a person tends to be stingy, think of him as he is going to be when he is more generous. Then when you see him being generous (and you will, if you are looking for it), you can comment that he is a generous person for doing that or that it was a generous act. This makes that person want to fulfill your expectations of him. He thinks, "She thinks I am generous so I better not disappoint her." Most likely, the person will become more generous because you bring out the best in him.

Many times, people will do just the opposite when trying to help others change. They perceive a weakness in someone (stinginess, for example) and bring it to his attention, thinking that they are doing that person a favor. Unfortunately, this is seen as a control issue, and the person simply puts up resistance to change. He just pushes back and perhaps makes a rude comment in reply. It is incredible how people think you don't know your own weaknesses and must be reminded of them! When this happens, we become upset with ourselves for not being able to overcome that weakness, and then this is transferred to the other person because they are judging you on the two percent that you are least proud of.

This happens frequently during performance reviews. The amazing thing is that the reviewer can't understand why people don't change more when all of their faults and shortcomings are pointed out during every review. This same reviewer will also most likely set new, ever-higher goals and objectives for the person, which further prevents change. This old method of reward and punishment to make people change doesn't work in the long run. Rather, it produces cynical, go-through-the-motions people who know that no matter how well they do their job, no one will be satisfied, and the bar will be raised even higher.

In order to really help people change and overcome their weaknesses, it is important to treat them as having already changed and stress their strengths. Most weaknesses are simply strengths taken to an extreme. A service-oriented person, for example, is warm and friendly, but talks too much and can't get the work done, or a salesman is so busy making new sales calls that he doesn't have time to make follow-up contacts. To help people change, it is best to stress their strengths and let them name the areas where they want to show improvement. After hearing what they are doing right, the people feel free to share some areas of weakness. If the performance reviewer can see the person as having already overcome a weakness, he can comment on a specific time when that weakness wasn't present. Finding an exception to the norm helps a person realize that he isn't that way "all the time."

Some people spend their whole life trying to overcome their weaknesses. This can sometimes lead to a frustrating existence because no matter how hard they try, there are some areas in their life that they cannot improve upon. Instead of trying to overcome these areas, the secret is to simply manage them so they won't impact life in a negative way. Stressing strengths, while managing weaknesses, is a key to positive change.

An example here might be helpful. One of my clients was a man who started and developed a very successful business. He was from a very large family, and many of his extended relatives asked to work in his business. Being a kind-hearted man, he just couldn't say no and hired practically the whole family. The business thrived for a time, but as soon as the relatives found out that they wouldn't be fired, the business started to decline. Even though the owner knew what was happening, he couldn't fire his relatives, and the company ultimately failed. Although my client was a good businessman, he couldn't manage his weakness of employing incompetent relatives.

People are able to change when they feel good about themselves and are positive about the future. Conversely, they resist change when they have a negative self-image and view the future as negative. By viewing a person as already having changed for the better and treating him that way, you can help him develop a positive self-image and a willingness to change.

CHAPTER 10:

TOUGH CASES

Sometimes, despite all your best efforts, people either can't or won't change. Either a behavior is so engrained that it has become part of their personality, or an addiction to a behavior or substance has formed. Addiction affects the desire to change and the rate of change. This is especially true when the change will in some way affect the addictive behavior.

Take the case of the woman who was ruining her relationships with her three younger siblings. When her mother died suddenly, she took on the responsibilities of a substitute mother and raised her siblings. This was a struggle for her, but she dedicated her life to their well-being and never married. Now, her siblings are married and have children of their own. They are a close family and interact often.

The conflict is that whenever she is around her siblings, she reminds them of all she did for them in the past. She tells them of the sacrifices she made, some of which they can't even remember. Her brothers and sisters are tired of this dialogue and just want to move on with their lives. They have told her repeatedly that they are grateful for what she did, but they don't want her to bring it up anymore. She is very aware of how they feel, but she can't seem to stop. She feels that they can't possibly appreciate her sacrifices, and so she keeps bringing them up at every opportunity.

Her siblings finally told her that if she persisted in this behavior, they would rather not be around her. Now she risked alienation from her brothers and sisters, who she loves, because she can't bring herself to change.

In this type of case, it is hard to help her change because she is stuck in the past. Using the ZG method, her siblings could ask her the miracle question to help her focus more on the future and could share their miracle day with her, explaining how it would be different if they were getting along better. They could also use the exception question and ask her about the times they were appreciative in the past. As always, the key is to persist in using the ZG method until the relationship improves.

In other tough cases, helping someone change could include breaking an addiction. The reason people engage in addictive behavior is to change how they feel. If people feel anxious, they may temper it through alcohol. In many ways, addiction is an escape from unpleasant realities and dysfunctional relationships. For example, a person would rather be drinking in a bar with strangers than be at home with his spouse. When using the ZG method to resolve conflicts, I have often noticed that addictive behavior decreases. I am not saying that using the ZG method cures addictions, but as relationships improve, people feel better about themselves and don't have as much reason to escape or change how they feel. As people repair relationships and relearn how to interact with others, they begin to feel good about themselves and their relationships. They don't need to feel different, so addictive behavior diminishes.

As we have seen when using the ZG method, when helping people change, you have to be willing to change first before the addicted person can change. Even though you have seen the person backslide before, you must be open to real, permanent change and just believe that this time it will be different. As healthy relationships improve, addictive behavior usually diminishes, sometimes to the point where it no longer interferes with normal activities and interactions. In these cases, the ZG method helps lead people away from isolation and indifference toward interaction and caring. People learn again to look outward and feel good about themselves. When a person feels good, there is no need for the comfort that addictive behaviors provide.

When presented with tough cases where the person won't change or where addiction is involved, it is important not to lose hope. Sometimes, major changes take time. It is comforting to know that using the ZG method correctly will not cause harm to a person. The ZG method helps people think about change in a way that is positive and nonthreatening. It opens the lines of communication and plants seeds of thought that may not sprout right away. At times, when confronted with challenging changes, you might think the method didn't work, but it is most important to give the ZG method your best effort because positive change may appear at a later time.

CHAPTER 11:

CONCLUSION

Vince Lombardi, the great Green Bay Packers coach, is often quoted as saying, "Winning isn't everything. It's the only thing." In many ways, the same can be said about good relationships—they are the only thing. The key in life isn't what we accomplish or how rich, popular, and powerful we are. It is the relationships we make along the way that are important, because they are some of the few things that have lasting value.

As we go through life, other things can seem more important. Money and what it will buy is often an obsession, but it can be fleeting, lost in a financial downturn. Money can also be isolating. What good is a fancy yacht or a mansion on a hundred acres if you don't have anyone to share it with?

Fame is also fleeting, as evidenced by old movie stars who have a lot more in common with other old people than with current movie stars. Eventually, people don't ask for their autograph, and then they don't even recognize them. The powerful people who retire or leave public office are left with a room full of pictures of themselves with other powerful people, who they never really had a relationship with.

We all know the importance of maintaining good relationships in close settings, such as with a spouse or other family members. But other relationships are also important. Trust and confidence are essential elements in every business relationship, whether you are on the phone making deals worth millions or getting your oil changed. Community relationships are also important because you need the community much more than the community needs you.

You can tell when people have difficulty forming and keeping good relationships because they keep changing spouses, houses, jobs, and communities. I was conducting a marriage seminar a few years ago when a man who was having marriage difficulties asked me how long I had been married. When I told him over thirty-five years, he said, "Oh. You must have found one of those good ones." I told him that a good marriage starts with *being* a "good one" rather than in finding a good one. This is also true in all relationships.

As we have seen throughout this short journey in resolving conflicts and building relationships, it all starts with you being one of those good ones. Your willingness to change and really work on improving your relationships will return immense dividends in your quality of life. This isn't always easy, and many obstacles will be in your way, including your own feelings. But you can accomplish the art of relationship-building and be better off for it. One day, I was complaining about my golf game to my son, and he said, "Dad, golf is just an excuse to hang out." He was right. When you have good relationships, the most fun and memorable times you will have is when you are just hanging out.

I hope this book has been a help to you in understanding how to resolve conflicts, how people change, and most importantly how to help them change. The method I have outlined has worked for me in helping many people solve their relationship difficulties. I have used it with hundreds of people in different settings over the past fifteen years. I have seen it work in families, marriages, and businesses. After using these steps, people come back together and start to work in a collaborative effort again so their families, marriages, and businesses can prosper. What's more, many people who have had success with this method pass it on to their families and co-workers. The simplicity and openness of the ZG method help people use it to create a changed, friendly environment where they live and work.

Now it is time for you to try the ZG method and see if it will work for you. Who doesn't want better relationships? The ZG method works because it is nonthreatening, positive, and future-oriented—like describing your own fairy tale. So go ahead. Take a chance and try it.

I'll bet you will be surprised.

Appendix I:

Scaling Questions

1) On a scale of one to ten, where is your relationship on the scale right now?

    1   2   3   4   5   6   7   8   9   10

    Worst ever   Best ever

2) Where on the scale would you need to be to feel satisfied in this relationship?

    1   2   3   4   5   6   7   8   9   10

    Not satisfied   Very satisfied

3) How willing are you to do your part to help make your relationship better?

    1   2   3   4   5   6   7   8   9   10

    Not willing to do anything   Will do almost anything

4) How confident are you that if you do your part, your relationship will be better?

    1   2   3   4   5   6   7   8   9   10

    Not confident   Very confident

5) In connection with this relationship, how do you feel about yourself right now?

    1   2   3   4   5   6   7   8   9   10

    Worst ever   Best ever

6) How do you feel about the answer to the previous question?

    1   2   3   4   5   6   7   8   9   10

    Feel real bad   Feel real good

Appendix II:

Scaling Questions Answer Sheet for Bob and Sue

SUE:

Where is your relationship on the scale right now?

Worst ever   Best ever

Session #1	1	<u>2</u>	3	4	5	6	7	8	9	10
Session #2	1	2	3	<u>4</u>	5	6	7	8	9	10
Session #3	1	2	3	4	5	<u>6</u>	7	8	9	10

Where on the scale would you need to be to feel satisfied in this relationship?

Not satisfied   Very satisfied

Session #1	1	2	3	4	5	6	<u>7</u>	8	9	10
Session #2	1	2	3	4	5	6	<u>7</u>	8	9	10
Session #3	1	2	3	4	5	6	<u>7</u>	8	9	10

How willing are you to do your part to help make your relationship better?

Not willing   Will do anything

Session #1	1	2	3	4	5	6	7	8	<u>9</u>	10
Session #2	1	2	3	4	5	6	7	8	<u>9</u>	10
Session #3	1	2	3	4	5	6	7	8	<u>9</u>	10

<u>SUE</u> (Continued)

How confident are you that if you do your part, your relationship will be better?

Not confident   Very confident

Session #1 1 2 3 4 5 6 <u>7</u> <u>8</u> 9 10

Session #2 1 2 3 4 5 6 7 <u>8</u> 9 10

Session #3 1 2 3 4 5 6 7 8 <u>9</u> 10

In connection with this relationship, how do you feel about yourself right now?

Worst ever   Best ever

Session #1 1 2 <u>3</u> 4 5 6 7 8 9 10

Session #2 1 2 3 <u>4</u> <u>5</u> 6 7 8 9 10

Session #3 1 2 3 4 5 6 <u>7</u> 8 9 10

How do you feel about the answer to the previous question?

Feel real bad   Feel real good

Session #1 <u>1</u> 2 3 4 5 6 7 8 9 10

Session #2 1 2 3 <u>4</u> 5 6 7 8 9 10

Session #3 1 2 3 <u>4</u> 5 6 7 8 9 10

<u>BOB</u>:

Where is your relationship on the scale right now?

Worst ever   Best ever

Session #1 1 2 3 <u>4</u> <u>5</u> 6 7 8 9 10

Session #2 1 2 3 4 <u>5</u> <u>6</u> 7 8 9 10

Session #3 1 2 3 4 5 6 7 <u>8</u> 9 10

Where on the scale would you need to be to feel satisfied in this relationship?

Not satisfied   Very satisfied

Session #1 1 2 3 4 5 <u>6</u> <u>7</u> 8 9 10

<u>BOB</u> (Continued)

Session #2	1	2	3	4	5	6	<u>7</u>	8	9	10
Session #3	1	2	3	4	5	6	7	<u>8</u>	9	10

How willing are you to do your part to help make your relationship better?

Not willing   Will do anything

Session #1	1	2	3	4	5	6	7	8	9	<u>10</u>
Session #2	1	2	3	4	5	6	7	8	9	<u>10</u>
Session #3	1	2	3	4	5	6	7	8	9	<u>10</u>

How confident are you that if you do your part, your relationship will be better?

Not confident   Very confident

Session #1	1	<u>2</u>	3	4	5	6	7	8	9	10
Session #2	1	2	3	<u>4</u>	5	6	7	8	9	10
Session #3	1	2	3	4	5	<u>6</u>	7	8	9	10

In connection with this relationship, how do you feel about yourself right now?

Worst ever   Best ever

Session #1	1	2	3	4	<u>5</u>	6	7	8	9	10
Session #2	1	2	3	4	<u>5</u>	6	7	8	9	10
Session #3	1	2	3	4	5	6	<u>7</u>	8	9	10

How do you feel about the answer to the previous question?

Feel real bad   Feel real good

Session #1	1	2	<u>3</u>	4	5	6	7	8	9	10
Session #2	1	2	3	4	<u>5</u>	6	7	8	9	10
Session #3	1	2	3	4	5	6	<u>7</u>	8	9	10

Sample Answer Sheet for You

Using an answer sheet similar to this one helps you track your progress over time. Circle where you are on the scale during each session.

Where is your relationship on the scale right now?

	Worst									Best ever
Session #1	1	2	3	4	5	6	7	8	9	10
Session #2	1	2	3	4	5	6	7	8	9	10
Session #3	1	2	3	4	5	6	7	8	9	10

Where on the scale would you need to be to feel satisfied in this relationship?

	Not satisfied								Very	satisfied
Session #1	1	2	3	4	5	6	7	8	9	10
Session #2	1	2	3	4	5	6	7	8	9	10
Session #3	1	2	3	4	5	6	7	8	9	10

How willing are you to do your part to help make your relationship better?

	Not willing						Will	do	anything	
Session #1	1	2	3	4	5	6	7	8	9	10
Session #2	1	2	3	4	5	6	7	8	9	10
Session #3	1	2	3	4	5	6	7	8	9	10

How confident are you that if you do your part, your relationship will be better?

	Not confident							Very	confident	
Session #1	1	2	3	4	5	6	7	8	9	10
Session #2	1	2	3	4	5	6	7	8	9	10
Session #3	1	2	3	4	5	6	7	8	9	10

Sample Answer Sheet for You (Continued)

In connection with this relationship, how do you feel about yourself right now?

	Worst ever									Best ever
Session #1	1	2	3	4	5	6	7	8	9	10
Session #2	1	2	3	4	5	6	7	8	9	10
Session #3	1	2	3	4	5	6	7	8	9	10

How do you feel about the answer to the previous question?

	Feel real bad									Feel real good
Session #1	1	2	3	4	5	6	7	8	9	10
Session #2	1	2	3	4	5	6	7	8	9	10
Session #3	1	2	3	4	5	6	7	8	9	10

Appendix III:

Sample Questions for Use at Home

Milking the Scaling Questions

- Your answer on the first scaling question was a ____. What could happen to move that relationship up one half of a point to a ____?

- What could you do to bring the relationship up one half of a point?

- What can your spouse/boss/co-worker/parent/friend do to bring your relationship up one half of a point?

- What is the highest you have ever been? Describe the time when you were at your highest.

- What is working in the relationship right now? What is the strongest aspect of the relationship?

Miracle Question

- If a miracle happened tonight while you were sleeping and all the problems that brought you here to this point in your relationship were suddenly solved, what would be different?

Milking the Miracle Question

- Are any parts of the miracle happening now? If so, which ones?

- What could you do to help bring this miracle day about?

- What are you doing now to help bring this miracle about?

- What could your boss/spouse/parent/co-worker/family do to help bring this miracle about?

- What could I do to help bring this miracle about?

- Has your boss/spouse/parent/co-worker/family recently done any of the things you listed to help bring this miracle about?

- Has your boss/spouse/parent/co-worker/family ever done any of the things you listed to help bring this miracle about?

- When the relationship first started, did you do any of the things described in the miracle? If so, what things?

- Have you recently done any of the things described in the miracle? If so, what things?

Visualization Questions

- If suddenly your spouse/boss/child turned into the perfect spouse/boss/child, in what ways would *you* change?

- What will your marriage/workplace/relationship look like when it is the best it can be?

- What will your marriage/workplace/relationship sound like when it is the best it can be?

- How will you feel differently when your marriage/workplace/relationship is the best it can be?

- What would be happening to make you feel differently?

Substance-Abuse Treatment Questions

- If the problems in your relationship were suddenly resolved, what would you do with all the time you have been spending on fixing or worrying about the situation? Describe what you would do instead.

- When your relationship is happier, what will you be able to do that you aren't doing now?

- What, if anything, might present a challenge to your taking steps to improve your relationships this week? How will you meet the challenge?

Exception Question

- Describe a time in the past when your relationship was really great. What was different?

Additional Questions

- How would you know that your relationship has started to improve even a little bit?

- As far as this relationship is concerned, what would you like to see happen now?

- What can you do to bring out the best in your spouse/boss/child?

- What can you do to bring out the best in yourself?

Appendix IV:

Typical Marriage Session with Bob and Sue Using the ZG Method

SESSION ONE

Sue has felt for some time that she and Bob were drifting apart. She purchased a copy of *Better Than a Stick in the Eye* and decided to try the ZG method to see if it would strengthen their marriage and bring them back together. Bob and Sue have been married for sixteen years and have three children: two boys, aged eleven and nine, and a girl who is seven.

To prepare for the session, Sue has read and answered the six scaling questions and has recorded her answers. She has also asked herself the miracle question and has outlined her miracle day. In addition, she has answered the question about what she could do to help herself go up half a point on the first scaling question. For a week, Sue has done a few things from her miracle day, done a few things from her half-point list, and thought about some other questions pertaining to her relationship. Now, she is ready to talk with Bob.

When Bob comes home from work, Sue says, "Bob, would you have some time for me after dinner?"

Bob replies, "Sure."

After dinner, when the children are in their rooms doing homework, Sue says, "Bob, can you spare a few minutes?"

Bob replies "Sure," then Sue asks, "Could you turn off the TV, please?" and Bob obliges.

Sue: On a scale of one to ten, with ten being the best it can be, and one being the worst, where do you think our relationship is right now?

Bob: About a four or five.

Sue: Where on this scale would you need to be to be satisfied in our marriage?

Bob: About a six or seven.

Sue: That is about a two-point spread from where you are to where you need to be, right?

Bob: Yes, that is right—for some reason, I don't think our marriage is that bad.

Sue: How willing are you to do your part to help make things better?

Bob: I will do anything.

Sue: So on a scale of one to ten, with ten meaning you would do anything, you would be a ten.

Bob: Right.

Sue: If you do your part to help make our marriage better, how confident are you that it will actually get better? A one means you aren't confident at all, and a ten means you are very confident.

Bob: About a two. Nothing seems to help.

Sue: In connection with our marriage, how do you feel about yourself right now? A one means you feel real bad, and a ten means you feel real good.

Bob: Somewhere in the middle. About a five.

Sue: How do you feel about your answer to the previous question?

Bob: I would like to feel better.

Sue: The scale goes from one—you feel bad about being a five—to ten—you feel real good about being a five.

Bob: I guess I feel about a three being a five.

Sue: Thanks, Bob. Can I tell you where I am on the scales?

Bob: Sure.

Sue: On the first question about where our relationship is right now, I would say it is about a two. For me to be satisfied in our marriage relationship, I would need to be about a seven.

Bob: That is about the same as me, right?

Sue: That is right, but I need to go up five points. On the question about how willing I am to do my part to help make things better, I am about a nine.

Bob: I am a ten, so we both are willing to do our parts.

Sue: It seems so. With regard to the question about how confident I am that things would actually get better if I do my part, I am about a seven or eight. I am a three about how I feel about myself right now, and I feel terrible about being a three. I would say I feel a one about being a three.

Bob: Why are you so low?

Sue: Let's not get sidetracked. I have a few more questions for you. Bob, let's just say that tonight while we are asleep, a miracle happens and as a result of that miracle, all the conflicts in our marriage are suddenly solved and our marriage is a ten, or a perfect marriage. If that happened, what would be different?

Bob: Wow. That would take a big miracle. What do you mean, "What would be different"?

Sue: Well, for example, what would happen differently when you first woke up in the morning after the miracle?

Bob: I'd be a millionaire because I won the lottery.

Sue: What else?

Bob: You'd be gone and I'd wake up next to a gorgeous supermodel.

Sue: Okay. If I wasn't gone, but had changed into the perfect wife, what would it be like? What would happen?

Bob: What day is this? Is it a work day or a weekend day?

Sue: Any day you want.

Bob: Well, let's say it is a work and school day.

Sue: Okay. What would be different?

Bob: Well, the alarm would go off as usual, and I would turn it off. Then I would wake you up because you don't hear the alarm. And if it was really a miracle day, you would get right up and get in the shower instead of just rolling over and falling back asleep.

Sue: Then what would happen?

Bob: Then I would go downstairs and make coffee as usual, and I would bring you a cup like I always do. When I got back to the bedroom, you wouldn't still be in bed, but would have finished your shower and, miracle of miracles, the bed would be made.

Sue: What would you say if that happened?

Bob: I would probably say thanks for making the bed and for getting in and out of the shower so I can use it.

Sue: Then what would happen the rest of this miracle day?

Bob: I would finish dressing while you went downstairs and started getting breakfast. And you would have time to get a second cup of coffee and some oatmeal before you got the kids up.

Sue: Then what would happen?

Bob: I would come down and get some cereal with the kids, and we would sit around the table and talk about the day. All the kids have different activities, so we would plan that. And you would have time to help them get ready for school.

Sue: Keep going.

Bob: Then you would take them to school, and I would go to work. There wouldn't be any last-minute crisis like usual.

Sue: Instead of a last-minute crisis, what would be happening?

Bob: Well, the kids would have all their homework done and be ready to go to school.

Sue: What else?

Bob: You wouldn't be in a bad mood on my miracle day.

Sue: If I was in a really good mood, how could you tell?

Bob: You wouldn't be complaining about my mother.

Sue: Instead of complaining, what would I be saying about your mother?

Bob: You would ask how she's doing and if I'm going to stop and see her after work.

Sue: What else would I be doing differently?

Bob: You would be nicer.

Sue: Okay, if that happened, how would you know? What would I be saying or doing differently so you would know that I was nicer?

Bob: You wouldn't bite my head off when I ask if you could run some errands after work. You would pack a lunch for me so I wouldn't have to stop on my route and buy lunch, and you would take a minute and really say goodbye, not just fly by with a half peck on the cheek.

Sue: Okay. So tell me more about your miracle day.

Bob: Work would go great. My truck would be running fine, and all my orders would be waiting for me. And I wouldn't have any emergency orders that would screw up my day.

Sue: How else would we interact during the day? Would you communicate with me?

Bob: Probably not, because, as you know, we aren't allowed to use our cell phones while we are driving, and I don't like to take the time to call because you are really busy at work and hard to get to. When I opened my lunch, though, there would be a note in there from you, saying "I love you."

Sue: Like the old days.

Bob: Right. I always enjoyed getting your notes.

Sue: Then what would happen?

Bob: I would finish up my route early because there wouldn't be any emergency deliveries, and I would stop by to visit Mom on the way home. Since Dad died, she gets lonely and needs company.

Sue: Then what would happen?

Bob: I would get home about the usual time. When I walked in, you and the kids would be doing homework around the table, and you would give me a hug and ask about my day.

Sue: Then what would happen? What else would be different?

Bob: Well, if this was really a miracle day, you would hand me a beer and the paper and say, "Why don't you go relax for a little while."

Sue: What else?

Bob: Then we would have dinner, and there wouldn't be any fighting or arguing.

Sue: Instead of fighting or arguing, what would we be talking about?

Bob: We all would be sharing our day with each other and talking about plans for the weekend. It would be a pleasant meal.

Sue: What would happen next?

Bob: I would help the kids with the homework they hadn't finished. Then we would watch a little TV.

Sue: Then what?

Bob: We would go up to bed, and the bedroom would be all picked up and the bed would be made.

Sue: What would you be thinking about as you went to sleep on your miracle day?

Bob: I would be so happy to have had a day with no arguing or disagreements, where everyone worked together to have a happy family. I would go to bed in peace.

Sue: Thanks, Bob, for sharing your miracle day with me. That was a great day. Would you like to hear about my miracle day?

Bob: Sure.

Sue: My miracle day would also be a work day like yours, Bob. I would know for sure that a miracle had happened because when the alarm went off, you wouldn't be such a grouch. Instead, you would say, "Good morning, honey," and I would say, "Good morning," too. Then you would go down to the kitchen and make coffee as usual. After that, you would come back upstairs and I would be out of the shower, and we would both get dressed. Then we would have about fifteen minutes to talk over coffee before we wake the kids. As part of the miracle, you would be in a good mood like you are on Saturdays, and we would talk about our plans for the day. As a matter of fact, we would set the alarm about fifteen minutes ahead so we would have time to talk. Then we would wake the kids, and, presto, the miracle has affected them too, and they are in a good mood. On my miracle day, we wouldn't be running around at the last minute looking for their homework or school clothes because they would have done all that the night before. And the conversation would be about things we are going to do on the weekend as a family and not so much complaining. Then you would go to work, and I would take the kids to school and then go to work. After getting started so well, my day would go very well. Everyone at work would get along. And you would even call me about ten o'clock. I know we would have to keep it short, but you would just ask me how my day was going, and you would tell me you love me. This would be like old times, too, because you used to do it all the time when we were first married and even before we were married. You always managed to call me at work sometime during the day, and I really looked forward to that. It made my day. Then, I would get all my work done and pick up the kids at school at four o'clock, and they would be all ready, waiting for me, with all their stuff—that would really be a miracle. Then we would go home, I would start dinner, and the kids would sit down at the kitchen table and do their homework. And on my miracle day, you wouldn't just come in, pop a beer, and go into the other room and read the paper. Instead, you would come in and sit with me and the kids, and we would talk about our day for about twenty minutes. Then, you would go read your paper while I finish dinner. After that, we would have a pleasant dinner with the whole family. The kids would finish their homework and get ready for school the next day. Then you and I would sit together on the couch and watch TV before we went to bed instead of you falling asleep in your chair. And before we turned off the light, I would be thinking about what a great day it was and how good it would be to have more miracle days. Thanks, Bob, for listening to my miracle day. I have to go now and help the kids get ready for bed.

SESSION TWO

One week after their first session using the ZG method, Sue has seen some improvement in their relationship. In the last week, Sue has been getting up a little earlier, making the bed and tidying the bedroom in the morning, and taking the time to give Bob a hug and a real kiss on the way out the door.

Sue also does her homework prior to the session. Even though some things have been worse since the last session, she stays positive and writes down all the things that have been better. Then, she revisits the scaling questions and compares her new answers to where she was last week. Sue is delighted to see that she has moved up a little on four of the questions. After that, she writes down all the things she could do to help herself move up on the scale and all the things Bob could do to help her move up.

Sue is almost ready for another conversation with Bob. She reviews the recommended question list for the second session. The first is the "What's better?" question. This question simply asks, "Since our conversation last week, is there anything in our relationship that has been better?" Then, she will ask the six scaling questions again. Next, she will ask Bob the half-point question, saying, "You see our relationship as a five. What could I do to raise that number a little bit, maybe a half of a point?" The fourth question is similar, asking, "What could you do to raise yourself a half of a point on the scale?"

She knows that it is very important to stick to these questions only and to stop when she has finished asking them. She will refrain from discussing the answers during or after the session and will not offer advice to Bob on what he could do to move himself up on the scale. After Sue has rehearsed the process and written everything down, she is ready to begin.

Sue: Bob, since our conversation last week, what do you think has been better about our relationship?

Bob: I don't know. That was a pretty bad argument we had last night.

Sue: We can get to that later. For now, I am mainly interested in hearing about anything that was better. It can be about our relationship, our family, or even about work.

Bob: I think you are really trying. You made the bed and picked up the bedroom three or four times last week. I know you are really busy with work, the kids, and all you do, but it is nice to see the bedroom looking good.

Sue: What else is better?

Bob: You've been getting up earlier, and the mornings seem a little calmer.

Sue: What else is better?

Bob: We had a great dinner last Friday. I appreciate your taking the time to do that.

Sue: Anything else better, Bob?

Bob: Not that I can think of.

Sue: Okay Bob, if you think of anything else that is better, you can mention it later. Would you like to hear about what I think is better?

Bob: Sure.

Sue: I think quite a bit has been better. That argument wasn't nearly as bad as some we've had. I agree with you that the mornings were a little calmer last week. I also think you have been trying a little harder. For instance, you've been in a better mood. And you have been a little better about coming home on time and helping the kids with their homework. The other thing that is better is your mother hasn't been calling as much. You know, sometimes she calls the house three or four times a day and always during dinner.

Bob: She is just lonely.

Sue: I know. Bob, I would like to ask you those same scaling questions I asked last week. Do you remember the ones where a one is the worst and a ten is the best?

Bob: Yes, I do.

Sue: On a scale of one to ten, where would you say our relationship is right now?

Bob: Oh, up about one from last week. Where was I last week?

Sue: You were a four and a half.

Bob: Okay, then, now I am a five and a half.

Sue: What made you go up this last week?

Bob: I think you are really trying.

Sue: And where on the scale would you need to be to feel satisfied for the long term?

Bob: About a seven.

Sue: And how willing are you to do your part to help make things better?

Bob: I am a ten.

Sue: And how confident are you that if you do your part, things will actually be better?

Bob: I am more confident now.

Sue: Last week you were a two.

Bob: Well, let's double that to a four.

Sue: What happened for you to double your confidence level?

Bob: You are trying. The bed is made.

Sue: Bob, in connection with our marriage, how do you feel about yourself right now?

Bob: About the same. What was I last week?

Sue: You were a five.

Bob: I am still a five—in the middle.

Sue: And how do you feel about being a five?

Bob: I feel okay about it. I am in the middle about being in the middle, if you know what I mean.

Sue: Sure. You feel a five about being a five. Would you like to hear where I am on the scales?

Bob: Sure.

Sue: On the scale of one to ten, I think our relationship right now is about a four. Last week I was about a two, so I have moved up two points. Where our marriage would need to be for me to be satisfied for the long term, I would be about a seven, which is the same as last week. On the question about how willing am I to do my part to help make things better, I am the same—about a nine. On the confidence scale that things will actually get better, I am pretty confident—about an eight. And I feel better about myself right now. I am a four and a half instead of a three. And I feel better about being a four and a half. I think there is hope now, so I feel about a four being a four and a half. That is up about three points.

Bob, you said you think our relationship is a five and a half. What could I do to raise that number a little bit? Say a half point or so.

Bob: One thing you could do is to keep your hobby stuff either out of our bedroom or put away in the closet. And you could make our bed every day.

Sue: If I did those two things, Bob, how much would you go up?

Bob: About a half point.

Sue: What else could I do?

Bob: You could cook a little more.

Sue: What do you mean?

Bob: It seems we have a lot of pizza, fast food, and frozen stuff. I would like a good home-cooked meal for dinner once in a while.

Sue: And how much would you go up if that happened?

Bob: Maybe a half point or even a whole point if you made one of your peach pies for dessert.

Sue: What else could I do to help you go up?

Bob: You could try to be more understanding about Mom. This first year without Dad has been hard, and there are some things I have to do for her that my sisters can't.

Sue: If I was more understanding about your mom, how much would you go up?

Bob: At least a whole point—maybe even two.

Sue: What else could I do to help you go up?

Bob: You could try to curb your hobby stuff a little. The basement is full. The bedroom closet is full, and it is expensive.

Sue: If this happened, how far up would you go?

Bob: At least two points minimum.

Sue: What else could I do to help you go up on the scale?

Bob: I can't think of anything else. If just the stuff I mentioned would happen, I would be a ten-plus.

Sue: Thank you, Bob. Would you like to hear about some things that you could do that would help me go up on the scale?

Bob: Sure.

Sue: Well, you could help out more around the house and with the kids. If you see a full basket of clean laundry sitting in the utility room, you could bring it up. If you took the laundry upstairs without being asked, I would go up about half a point. You could also clean up after yourself better. Like if you have a drink and a snack on Saturday afternoon, you could take the dirty dishes back to the kitchen. That would help me go up another half point. And I would go up another half point if you would help out with the kids' homework after dinner, especially in math. I think I would go up a whole point

if you could limit the time you spend with your mom.
I know she is a new widow, but sometimes I think you
spend more time over there than here. This last one is
bigger: I would go up two points if on boys' night out,
you would come home on time or call, and you would
cut back on your drinking.

I have just one more question for you. What are some
things you could do to help yourself go up on the scale
to enhance our relationship?

Bob: I guess one thing I could do is to keep talking with
you like this. I think maybe it is helping us.

Sue: What else could you do to go up or enhance our
marital relationship?

Bob: I could stop finding fault with you and the children.
Sometimes, I just fly off for no good reason about
nothing.

Sue: What else could you do?

Bob: I could stop arguing, especially with you. In fact, I
made up my mind to just not argue anymore.

Sue: How are you going to do that, Bob?

Bob: Well, I haven't figured it all out yet. I guess I just
won't say anything so there won't be an argument. Then
maybe later we can just discuss it.

Sue: It sounds like you have been thinking about this.

Bob: Yes. I really hate to argue, especially with you. It seems
like it brings out the worst in us, and it is really hard
on the kids.

Sue: What else could you do?

Bob: That is about it for now.

Sue: Can I tell you some things I could do to go up or
enhance our relationship?

Bob: Sure.

Sue: One thing I could do would be to stop yelling,
especially at the boys. It doesn't seem to help, anyway.

It would be a lot quieter around the house, and maybe everyone else would quiet down. I could also try to be happier and at peace with things. And finally, I could get hopeful that our marriage is really going to last and not lose heart over some of the things that seem major but probably aren't. Thanks for listening, Bob. I enjoyed our time together. Now I have to check on the kids before they go to bed.

SESSION THREE

Sue has been feeling better about her improving relationship with Bob. In the last week, she has continued getting up earlier, making the bed and tidying the bedroom in the morning, and taking the time to give Bob a hug and a real kiss on the way out the door. She has added two more things this week—making a big dinner on Sunday and cleaning up the basement. Sue has noticed that Bob has been more helpful around the house and had less to drink the last time he went out with the boys.

Sue would like to have one more session, so she does her homework. By now, she is comfortable with the questions, writing down what's better and using her scoring sheet for the six scaling questions. In addition, she selects ten more questions from the list in Appendix III and writes down her answers. She selects the following questions:

- Is there anything the kids could do to help me move up on the scale?

- What could my mother-in-law do to help bring my miracle day about?

- If Bob suddenly turned into the perfect husband, how would I change?

- What do I think is the highest score our relationship has ever been?

- If I were a fly on the wall in our house now, what would be different than it was two weeks ago? What would I be hearing that would be different? What would look different?

- As far as our marriage relationship is concerned, what would I like to see happen now?

- What, if anything, might present a challenge to us continuing to move in the right direction?

- How will I feel differently when our marriage is a ten?

- If the miracle happened and all of our problems were solved, what would I do with all the time I have been spending worrying about the situation?

- What can Bob do to bring out the very best in me, and what I can do to bring out the best in him?

Sue starts the conversation by asking Bob what has been better since their last talk.

Bob: I think the best thing that happened was our little date. I just wanted you to know how special you are to me, and that's why I planned it. Sending the kids to Mom's house made it feel like a night just for us.

Sue: Bob, it was wonderful! That was number one on my list of what is better, too. I can't believe you planned the whole thing without me knowing about it. And suggesting that I relax while you picked up the kids finished a perfect date. After that, I really felt like I had the old Bob back.

Bob: It is interesting you say that because I was thinking that I finally got the old Sue back, too.

Sue: Is anything else better?

Bob: I appreciated it when you invited Mom over for dinner, and the dinner of meatloaf, mashed potatoes, fresh green beans, and homemade peach pie was a real treat. Then Mom watched the kids while we went to a movie. It was another great night.

Sue: Is anything else better?

Bob: The basement looks great since you organized it and put up a curtain to hide your hobby stuff. I feel like I can take my buddies down there now.

Sue: Is anything else better, Bob?

Bob: No. That is about it.

Sue: Actually, I have one more thing that is better. When you went out with the guys the other night, you came home on time, and I could tell you hadn't had much to drink. I really appreciated that. Now, I would like to ask you the same scaling questions. On a scale of one to ten, where is our marriage relationship now?

Bob: Right now, after two good weeks, it is about an eight.

Sue: That is up about two and a half points over a week ago and up three and a half points over our initial talk.

Bob: Things are definitely better now.

Sue: Bob, where on the scale would you need to be to have a satisfying marriage over the long term?

Bob: About an eight.

Sue: That is up one from last week.

Bob: I guess I have raised my expectations about what our marriage can be over the long term.

Sue: And how willing are you to do your part to help make our marriage better?

Bob: I am still a ten.

Sue: How confident are you that if you do your part, things will actually get better?

Bob: I am now a six. I think that is up from last time.

Sue: Yes. It's up two points from a four at our last talk like this and up four points from a two a few weeks ago. You seem more confident now.

Bob: In the past when I would try, nothing seemed to work, but now things are working better.

Sue: Can you tell me what is working better?

Bob: Well, for example, our little date. I think you really enjoyed that.

Sue: Bob, how do you feel about yourself right now?

Bob: About a seven.

Sue: That is up from a five at our last conversation.

Bob: When things are better at home, I feel better about myself.

Sue: How do you feel about being a seven?

Bob: I feel a seven about being a seven.

Sue: Thanks. Would you like to hear where I am on the scales? On the first scale, where is our relationship now, I am about a six. It could be higher, but I need to see if this is going to last. So, on this question, I am up four points from when we started and up two points from a week ago. On the scale about where I would need to be to feel satisfied over the long term, I am about a seven. That is the same as the last two times. And on the scale about how willing I am to do my part to help make things better, I am about a nine. That is the same as the last two times, too. On the scale about how confident I am that if I do my part things will be better, I am a nine. I feel a little more confident. On that question, I am up one point over last week and up one and a half points over our first talk. With regard to the question about how I feel about myself right now, I feel a lot better—about a seven. In these last two weeks, I feel that you really showed that you care about me. That is up from a three when we first started and up from a four and a half from a week ago. I have moved up quite a bit in this category. I feel a lot better about myself now, and I feel good about being a seven. Sometimes in the past, I thought I would never be a seven again. I probably feel a seven about being a seven.

Is there anything the kids could do to help you move up on the scale?

Bob: It would be helpful if they would clean up their rooms and put their stuff away. Sometimes when I come home, there is so much sports stuff lying around the driveway and in the garage that I can't even get the car in. I have to get out and move stuff just to park the car in the garage.

Sue: Anything else?

Bob: Well, if they could just do that, it would be a major improvement.

Sue: For me, the kids could do their chores without me nagging them about it.

Remember your miracle day? What could your mother do to bring your miracle day about?

Bob: I know I am spending a lot of time with Mom, but a lot of it has to do with settling the estate and finding someone to run the farm. When all this is finally settled in a couple of months, my sisters can help Mom more, and I won't have to put in so much time. But Mom did entertain the kids while we had our date, and maybe we could have her watch the kids more so we can be alone.

Sue: When I think about what your mom could do to help my miracle day, I would say she wouldn't call as often and wouldn't give me so much advice about the kids. Instead, she would call your sisters sometimes and would tell me that I am a great mom. Actually, your mom doesn't bother me as much anymore. In all fairness, the kids really enjoy being with her and visiting the farm. And she is open to watching the kids for us when we want to do special things together. I guess, in some ways, she is helping my miracle come about.

If I suddenly turned into the perfect wife, how would you change?

Bob: You know, when we were first married, I thought you were the perfect wife for me. Then, we kind of drifted apart over the years. But in the last two weeks, I feel like I have the old Sue back. We have been laughing and joking like the old days. I guess I would be more involved with family stuff and let you know more that I love you. Until last Saturday, I didn't realize how much you worry about stuff.

Sue: I have been thinking about the old Sue, too. The old Sue was pretty carefree. I didn't worry about stuff like I do now. It seemed like I had more time for me. Now I feel like I am in this whirlwind, spinning around, trying to juggle the kids, you, your mom, the house, bills, and everything else. For our date, you took charge of everything, and all I had to do was just go along. That is the way you used to be. I didn't have to worry about anything, and the old Sue came out. You got your mom to watch the kids, chilled the wine, and planned a wonderful meal for us. The old Bob did stuff like that all the time when we were dating and even when we were first married.

I think our relationship was a ten when we were first married. What do you think was the highest we have ever been?

Bob: A ten-plus when we were first married.

Sue: Yes, definitely. We really had fun together back then. I have been thinking about how I would change if you suddenly became perfect. I guess I wouldn't worry so much. When things aren't going well, I worry all the time. I even have trouble going to sleep some nights.

So if you were perfect, you would be taking care of stuff, and I wouldn't have to worry anymore.

If I were a fly on the wall in our house now, what would be different than it was two weeks ago? What would I be hearing that would be different?

Bob: You wouldn't hear any arguing now and not many loud voices from the kids. The whole household seems quieter now.

Sue: If I wouldn't be hearing that, what would I be hearing?

Bob: Peace and quiet. If the whole family was there, we would probably be talking about our plans for the weekend.

Sue: I was thinking what would look different to the fly now rather than two weeks ago. The whole house is picked up and straighter. There aren't any boxes of snacks or plates sitting around anymore. You really got on the kids about this, and things have improved. As far as our marriage is concerned, what would you like to see happen now?

Bob: I would like to see it keep getting better.

Sue: How would that happen?

Bob: You and I would have to continue to do the things we have been doing.

Sue: What, if anything, might present a challenge to us continuing to move in the right direction?

Bob: The biggest challenge is not letting our relationship slip back to what it was—where it was just on automatic.

Sue: What do you plan to do to keep this from happening?

Bob: I plan to make more time when we can really connect with each other. I am also going to continue to not argue and try to maintain a good level of communication between us. I want to put our relationship first and stop taking it for granted. If things get bad again, we can go back to these questions, but I am hoping we won't have to.

Sue: I have been thinking about how I will feel differently when our marriage is a ten again. When I feel like the old Sue is around all the time, then I will know that our marriage is a ten. I won't be so worried, and I will smile and laugh more. I will feel more at ease around you because I could say anything that I was thinking about without you getting upset. When our relationship is a ten, I will be able to sleep better. I guess I could just be myself, too. I have been trying so hard to keep everything together that I didn't have time to just be the old Sue. If the miracle happened and all of our problems were solved, I would probably have the time and inclination to start my exercise program again. It seems like the last few months, I just haven't felt like doing any exercising. I would call up Cindy and see if she wanted to walk like we have done in the past. She has called me a few times recently, but I haven't felt like walking. Bob, if your miracle happened, how would you feel and what will you be able to do that you aren't doing now?

Bob: I'd definitely be happier. I'd be home more. I wouldn't need to get away from the chaos in the house because everything in the house will be calmer and more organized. So, I'd spend more time with you and the kids. I could even do things with just the kids so you could have a little more time to yourself.

Sue: Bob, what can you do to bring out the very best in me?

Bob: I guess I could try to understand you more. When we had our date that Saturday, just the two of us, I just sat and listened. You had a lot to say and I just listened. It was after that the old fun-loving Sue came out. I guess I could set the stage so that happens more often.

Sue: I have been thinking about what I can do to bring out the best in you. I think these question-and-answer sessions have been a big factor in helping both of us communicate better. For a long time, I didn't say anything and tried to work out things by myself, but that didn't work. When we tried to talk before, it seemed like we always ended up in an argument about things that had happened in the past, and our relationship got worse. Using these questions brought out the best in you. Now it seems like we can talk about important things in a quiet, nonemotional manner. And as things changed, we had a way to measure our progress so we knew our relationship was getting better. Now we have a method that can help us if things get bad again. Thanks for your help, Bob, in making this all work. Now I have to go check on the kids before they go to bed.

Appendix V:

Questions for Use at Work

Scaling Questions

1) How well is the company being run right now?

1   2   3   4   5   6   7   8   9   10

Worst ever   Best ever

2) How willing are you to do your part to help it run better?

1   2   3   4   5   6   7   8   9   10

Not willing to do anything at all   Will do almost anything

3) How confident are you that if you did your part, things would be better?

1   2   3   4   5   6   7   8   9   10

Not confident   Very confident

4) How do you feel about your work right now?

1   2   3   4   5   6   7   8   9   10

Worst ever   Best ever

5) How do you feel about the answer to the previous question?

1   2   3   4   5   6   7   8   9   10

Feel real bad   Feel real good

<u>Additional Questions</u>

- If a miracle happened and your company was being run the very best it could be—a ten or a perfectly running business—what would be different?
- What could you do to help bring this miracle about?
- What could other co-workers do to help bring this miracle about?
- What could your boss do to help bring this miracle about?
- Have any parts of this miracle ever happened in the past? If so, which ones?
- Are any parts of this miracle starting to happen right now? If so, which ones?
- If the miracle came about, how would you know it happened? What would it look like?
- Your answer on the first scaling question (How well is your company being run right now?) was a ___. What would have to happen to move it up half a point?
- What could you do to bring it up half a point?
- What could your co-workers do to bring it up half a point?
- What could your boss do to bring it up half a point?
- If suddenly your boss changed into the perfect boss, in what ways would you change?
- What will the company look like when the miracle happens and the company reaches its full potential?
- How will you feel differently about working here when the company reaches its full potential?

APPENDIX VI:

Typical Workplace Questionnaire and Summary Report Using the ZG Method

The following is an example of how the ZG method can be used in a formal large group. This company recently acquired another small company.

1) How well is the company being run right now? Avg. 5.23

1   2   3   4   <u>5   6</u>   7   8   9   10

Worst ever   Best ever

2) How willing are you to do your part to help it run better? Avg. 9.82

1   2   3   4   5   6   7   8   <u>9   10</u>

Not willing to do anything at all   Will do almost anything

3) How confident are you that if you did your part, things would be better? Avg. 8.4

1   2   3   4   5   6   7   <u>8   9</u>   10

Not confident   Very confident

4) How do you feel about your work right now? Avg. 7.00

1   2   3   4   5   6   <u>7</u>   8   9   10

Worst ever   Best ever

5) How do you feel about the answer to the previous question? Avg. 5.12

1   2   3   4   <u>5   6</u>   7   8   9   10

Feel real bad   Feel real good

Note: Numbers indicate how many team members gave each answer.

1) If a miracle happened and your company was being run the very best it could be—a ten or a perfectly running business—what would be different?

    11 - Delegation of authority and responsibility
    7 - Organized/procedures/paperwork flow/office policy
    7 - Communication better/know who to report to
    6 - Efficiency better/everyone knows job
    6 - Everyone would pull their weight
    2 - Attitude better
    1 - Service better

2) What could you do to help bring this miracle about?

    6 - Help organize
    5 - Accept change
    5 - Take responsibility
    3 - Be more involved
    3 - Help it come about
    2 - Do job best you know how
    1 - Be a cheerleader

3) What could other co-workers do to help bring this miracle about?

14 - Cooperate/teamwork

6 - Trust each other

3 - Make our own decisions/more responsibility

1 - Better attitude

1 - Accept change

1 - Better communication

4) **What could your boss do to help bring this miracle about?**

14 - Delegate

8 - Organize

4 - Communicate/listen

4 - No day-to-day responsibilities/concentrate on major decisions

3 - Help knit together both companies

1 - Accept mistakes

5) **Have any parts of this miracle ever happened in the past? If so, which ones?**

3 - When smaller/before acquiring other company

6) **Are any parts of this miracle starting to happen right now? If so, which ones?**

5 - We have gotten started

4 - Trying to help more

2 - Better attitude

1 - People starting to take more responsibility

7) **If the miracle came about, how would you know it happened? What would it look like?**

5 - Attitudes better

4 - More friendly atmosphere

4 - Running smoother and be easier

3 - Communication better

3 - People would be busier/not standing around

1 - Problems solved at a lower level

8) In regard to your answer on scaling question one (How well is your company being run right now?), what would have to happen to move it up half a point?

7 - Delegate responsibility

5 - Organizing

5 - Everyone be more relaxed and pulling together

2 - Start slow and work up (orderly progression)

2 - Job descriptions

9) What could you do to bring it up half a point?

5 - Help change happen

5 - Do more/get more involved

2 - Be more positive

2 - Be friendly to co-workers

10) What could your co-workers do to bring it up half of a point?

3 - Help change happen

3 - Work more efficiently

11) What could your boss do to bring it up half a point?

4 - Delegate

3 - Share vision

2 - Be more flexible

1 - Be more trusting/listen

12) If suddenly your boss changed into the perfect boss, in what ways would you change?

9 - Attitude change

6 - Take more responsibility/worry more

2 - Work habits change

2 - Do things better

1 - Pick up the pace

13) What will the company look like when the miracle happens and the company reaches its full potential?

3 - Have goals and objectives

3 - Managers not as much in day-to-day tasks

3 - Delegation

2 - Have meetings

2 - More timely and organized

2 - Better financially

14) How will you feel differently about working here when the company reaches its full potential?

12 - Happier

6 - Less frustrated/pressured

5 - More pride

3 - Appreciated more

3 - Proud of company

2 - More settled

2 - Better morale

1 - More energy

1 - Used to potential

1 - Go to a 10 personally

Summary and Recommendations

The answers to the scaling questions on the first part of the questionnaire are very important in determining where the company is, how willing the individual team members are to do their part, and how confident they are that they can make a difference. It also indicates how they feel about their work (self-image) and how they feel about the answer (self-esteem).

When we ask the scaling questions again in the future, it will help to determine the progress we are making.

The answer to question one was 5.23, which means that the team sees lots of room for improvement. Question two was 9.82, which is excellent because it means the work force is highly motivated. Question three was 8.41, which is excellent because the individual team members think they can make a difference. Question four was 7.00, which is good because it correlates with question one in that there is less than a difference of two points. It is important that questions one and four be close together to show that they really identify with how the company is doing. Question five, at 5.12, is very good because it shows a strong motivation for the individual to change.

In summary, conditions are excellent for improvement. The team is not happy with the status quo. They want to change; they believe they can change; and they believe they can change the company. They are ready to go, and from the responses to the other questions on the survey, they know how. As in all companies, the people working there know best what should be done.

For management to help make this come about, teams need to be formed who will address the changes that are needed. The results of the questionnaire indicate that the difficulties the company is having revolve around delegation, organization, cooperation, communication, and attitudes. In the team sessions, these topics will be expanded upon by milking the miracle question and the scaling questions that were asked in the original questionnaire. Each team will address an issue and formulate proposals to help the company attain its vision. Management will be a part of this team process to help facilitate the dialogue and arrive at workable solutions.

Using this system, all the important issues can be addressed with solutions implemented over time, and the teams will own the recommended outcomes.

APPENDIX VII:

Questions for Workplace Teams

- What is better?
- If, as a result of the miracle, delegation in our company was a ten, what would be different? What would people be doing differently?
- If, all of a sudden, everyone's attitude was better, how could you tell? What would they be saying so you would know it was better?
- If our company was organized the best it could be how would you know?
- If communication in our company was suddenly much better, what would people be saying to each other? How would they be responding to each other? What would you be hearing?
- If cooperation in our company was the best it could be, how could you tell? What would people be saying or doing differently? If you were an impartial observer, what would you be hearing that would lead you to the conclusion that the people in this company really cooperate?
- What are the strengths of our company?

- What are you doing to help the company be more productive and profitable?

- What could you do to help the company be more productive and profitable?

- What could your co-workers do?

- What could I [the boss] do to help you become more productive?

- What one thing could happen to really help our company?

- Can you describe what it is like when the team is having a really good day and everything is running smoothly?

- What, if anything, might present a challenge to enhancing the company's productivity and profitability? How can we meet this challenge?

- What would you like to see happen in your company now and in the future?

Printed in the United States
154525LV00005B/2/P

9 781438 986883